MY F-WORD IS FORGIVENESS

Herb Agee

WestBow
PRESS
A DIVISION OF THOMAS NELSON

WestBow Press books may be ordered through booksellers or by contacting:

WestBow Press
A Division of Thomas Nelson
1663 Liberty Drive
Bloomington, IN 47403
www.westbowpress.com
1-(866) 928-1240

Because of the dynamic nature of the Internet, any web addresses or links contained in this book may have changed since publication and may no longer be valid. The views expressed in this work are solely those of the author and do not necessarily reflect the views of the publisher, and the publisher hereby disclaims any responsibility for them.

Any people depicted in stock imagery provided by Thinkstock are models, and such images are being used for illustrative purposes only.

Certain stock imagery © Thinkstock.

ISBN: 978-1-4497-7053-2 (sc)
ISBN: 978-1-4497-7052-5 (e)
ISBN: 978-1-4497-7054-9 (hc)

Library of Congress Control Number: 2012921218

Printed in the United States of America

WestBow Press rev. date: 01/16/2013

TABLE OF CONTENTS

MY F-WORD IS FORGIVENESS

REV. HERB AGEE
(AKA PADRE)

PREFACE

his whole writing thing began to let the employees of Wuesthoff Hospital in Rockledge, Florida know that, after twelve years as their chaplain, I was leaving and why. Some people asked me if I would to continue to write after I left. They said they enjoyed the saga of the move enough to want to read more. I was flattered, amazed, and skeptical, especially skeptical. I thought they were just being nice. But so as not to miss an opportunity to write if it could be enjoyed or be a help in any way, I continued.

I began writing about the process of moving and the experiences of that adventure. I wrote for the next year to keep in touch with the ones I left behind. I later began writing as a guest on The Englewood Edge, a local online newspaper. Those stories make up the rest of this book.

CHAPTER 1—
CARDBOARD PURGATORY

Someone wrote and asked me where I've been the last few days and why I haven't written. Those of you who remember moving certainly know the answer. For those who have never moved, or it's been so long since a move, like a mother talking of labor pains and saying, "They weren't so bad," you have forgotten the agony, I'll tell you. The answer is: I've been in cardboard purgatory. This, of course, is very near cardboard you-know-where. If we don't get out of cardboard purgatory pretty quickly, I'm afraid we'll descend into that place of no return. You know, where you never really get completely unpacked, but always have some boxes with unknown contents lying around. You think you'll get to them eventually, but you never do. You think that maybe they contain the stuff you haven't been able to find yet, even though you sort of shuffled through them at some point and couldn't find anything important. They are the boxes in the attic or garage or shed or back in a closet somewhere that will eventually be moved again without ever being unpacked. They become a bizarre, eerie kind of time capsule of the life of your family, much like the film you find in a camera long since forgotten and considered lost forever with pictures of people whose names you don't remember. This brings questions like, "Honey, who is this and why did you take their picture?"

The other answers to "why haven't you written?" are: "I haven't had time with all the cleaning and unpacking," and "the computer wasn't set up yet." Would someone please explain how you can carefully pack everything from the computer into one or maybe two boxes; tape them securely shut, and yet have at least one necessary cable slither away to another box while riding in the truck? This phenomenon causes angry questions and statements, such as, "Who packed this in with these? You should know they don't go there?" or, "What idiot put these in here?" or, "Did a company of complete imbeciles pack for us?" These questions get more pointed and mean as the days drag on and cardboard purgatory takes its toll on your psyche.

My wife, Candy, used to say that a couple planning to get married should have to put up a Christmas tree together as part of the pre-marital counseling process. That's a project that will make those on-line personality tests look like you're playing hop-scotch to decide compatibility. Match.com or eharmony.com can never detect the difference in a person who just throws that silver spaghetti looking stuff on the tree, and one who carefully puts each of the hundreds or thousands of them in their individual place. But now, after this move, I think people who are considering marriage should have to pack up each other's things and unpack them again and see if they can stand the stress of losing important stuff without ever having taken it out of the apartment. I'm convinced that some boxes are from "The Twilight Zone." You put something in, close the box, open it again, and the thing you packed has either disappeared or changed into something you never knew you had and is completely useless. I am so glad that Candy and I have already made it through a few Christmas trees together. She's wonderful.

This reminds me of a Christmas several years ago, when we went to look for a tree together with Candy's son, Ross. Ross picked out a tree that was ten to twelve feet tall. Candy thought this size was unwise, even though we had a really high ceiling in the room waiting for the tree. My thinking was, "Christmas is for kids; let him pick the tree he wants."

Well, the tree fit fine and decorated beautifully with a unique combination of placing the silver things and eventually flinging them on the tree, because, "We'll never get this done if we have to place each one!!" Well, the next morning the branches had relaxed and it was a little wider, but it was still okay. The next morning they had spread out even more and by the third or fourth day, the tree was ten to twelve feet wide to match its height and we eventually had to pull it out to the middle of the room and sit on the couch with our feet up. It was impossible to see the television around the tree. We still laugh about that monster tree and we are still married, although we did buy an artificial tree the next year.

We're still cleaning and unpacking. Please stop what you are doing and say a special "get out of cardboard purgatory" prayer for us. And would you please emphasize that we especially need to be out by Christmas?

No one asked any more questions. I think they all understood.

CHAPTER 2--
BUSHES

We have gotten the house unpacked and together enough that Candy wants to start on the yard. She loves beauty and needs to have it around her. Evidently I don't quite fulfill that beauty need enough myself, so the only solution is to create some. I, personally, don't seem to have the same need for beautiful bushes and shrubs. Oh, don't get me wrong, I love walking through commercial gardens or looking at someone else's beautiful yard. The problem is: I am a man, and we seem to have some sort of x-ray vision when it comes to beautiful landscaping. We have the uncanny ability to see right through the beauty to the amount of work it took to make it happen.

Let me stop here to explain before anyone gets offended. I realize God creates the beauty, but somehow I seem to always get stuck with the grunt work. Now back to the yard.

Take a gorgeous bush for example. That didn't just pop up out of the ground like magic. There was either an empty spot on the ground, or worse yet, an old ugly bush taking up that space. To create beauty in that place involves first digging up the old bush, and please let me explain how that goes, not too good. When you first try to put your shovel in the ground, you find that someone in the past history of this yard thought it would be a good thing to put down four to six inches of decorative rock. This, at least in my opinion, is not a good thing.

Digging through rock is what John Henry did with his hammer, for those of you old enough to remember the song. Shovels are not made for that, but it's the only thing I have. I've never, before now, found the need to own a pick or jackhammer. So, using the shovel, you dig through the rock. Once you get to dirt, you feel confident this will go much better. That feeling lasts about two inches until you hit a root. Now, small roots from the bush itself are not really a problem for a sharp shovel. The key word here is sharp. Did I mention about digging through four inches of rock? Did you ever play "Rock, Paper, Scissors?" If I remember correctly, rock beats scissors. For future reference, rock beats shovel, too. But I'm rambling now.

What you thought was a small root from the bush turns out to be a huge root from a tree in the woods that is twenty feet away. I do own a chopping tool, but it seems to be way more effective on feet than on roots (but that's another story). After cutting out enough roots to start a small bonfire, you have a hole big enough for the bush. Now, you have to pull the new bush from the plastic pot in which it has grown for the last year or so. I'm guessing at this time period because the roots have not only grown through the little holes in the bottom and intertwined themselves, but somehow the plant has chemically bonded with the plastic, making it virtually impossible to pull apart. I don't understand how this happens, but neither chemistry nor botany was my major in seminary. So getting the plant out now requires another cutting tool, a razor knife, which moves the danger of injury from the feet to the hands. A razor knife…two sharp and dangerous ideas combined…who thought of this? By the way, it really hurts to scrub the dirt out of a nasty cut, and never show such a cut to your "doctor" wife who knows all about infections. Did you know that band-aids now come in decorator colors? Again, I ramble.

With the bush now cut free from the pot and all wounds cleaned and bandaged, you can actually plant the bush, which was the intent two hours ago when you began. It's beautiful! This remarkable process now fills you with a great sense of accomplishment until you realize that there are four more bushes to get in the ground. Isn't a beautiful yard a wonderful thing?

Whoever said, "Beauty is only skin deep" never did any landscaping.

CHAPTER 3-- FISHING

I went fishing at 6:00 am this morning with Clyde from next door. This meant getting up at 5:30, but don't ask me why. I can get ready for work in thirty minutes and that involves a shower, shampoo, shave (just the neck), brushed teeth, clean clothes, and various other things I don't want to talk about right now. Getting ready to go fishing involves putting on pants and a shirt and shoes, and any one of those is optional. That takes...let's see...I'm counting...something like forty-five seconds. So I'm ready twenty-nine minutes too early. This works for me, but for many men there is another problem to getting up early to go fishing. The real consumer of time on early fishing mornings is the "Honey, I was <u>trying</u> to be quiet" routine.

It's amazing how a man, who is typically unorganized, can prepare all his fishing gear the night before. This will include rods, reels, and tackle for any possible fishing situation. You never really know where you will end up; it just depends on where the fish are biting. So you take gear for fresh water, salt water, a mixture of salt and fresh, (odd, but important). You take every type of bait you could possibly use. This will include live things that will all be dead by the time you arrive, and artificial bait.

There are hundreds of types of lures which you need and the professional fishermen, who get paid by the companies which make them, gave you their solemn promise that each one will catch fish... guaranteed. You already know about artificial worms, because that slimy thing your son threw up in the air, which got stuck on the ceiling, was one of those. Don't worry, it usually only stays up there a month or two before it falls unsuspectingly on a guest, leaving a greasy stain where it had been stuck, which is as hard to clean as the stain left by your unsuspecting guest.

But, after preparing everything he might possibly need for fishing, the man goes to bed without getting his fishing clothes out and putting them in the garage or another room so he can dress without waking his wife. Waking her while getting dressed shouldn't be such a big deal; he already woke her every half hour since 3:00 am by using the flashlight to look at the clock to see how much longer before time to get up. He's like a kid waiting for his first trip to Disney. This is the same man she has to throw water on to get him up for work. But…evidently, it is a big deal that he awakens her while trying desperately to get dressed quietly. She speaks in that early morning voice…you know the one…the one that makes you wonder if you slept with Barry White. She says, "Hey, Baby." No, wait, that was Barry White. She really says, "Can't you be quiet?" To which the man lovingly responds, "Honey, I was trying to be quiet."

Why does he find it necessary to explain this to his "Sleeping Barry, uh, Beauty?"

Okay, here's how it goes. After checking the clock every half hour since 3:00, he falls asleep at 5:20 only to be awakened from a dream by the alarm at 5:30. After three or four rather noisy attempts at silencing the alarm while still not fully out of the dream, he finally gets it to stop. He lays back for a minute trying to remember why he needed to get up so early when suddenly it occurs to him, "I'm going fishing!!!" With that thought, he literally jumps out of the bed, leaving his wife bouncing up and down on her side. He then remembers that he needs to be quiet, so he tries to tiptoe around the bed. "How does that go?" you ask. I think you know the answer, not too good. He, of course, kicks the end of the bed, bending his little toe into a position which is only possible if you're that little double-jointed kid in school or by severe trauma. He then explodes with whispered expletives and does the injured toe dance which involves holding said toe and hopping around on the uninjured foot.

It has been scientifically proven that you cannot keep your balance while doing the injured toe dance and whispering expletives at the same time. You have to be able to scream expletives to keep your balance, but our considerate husband is still trying to be quiet; so he inevitably loses his balance and falls into the dresser, thus knocking over forty-two different bottles of perfume, cologne, body lotion, make-up and whatever else a woman uses to try to look and smell like somebody else. More whispered expletives brings further imbalance and he bumps back into the foot of the bed and falls on his wife's feet. Does she try to whisper her expletives? Let's not go there.

He quickly gets up and hobbles to the closet. They've probably lived in this house for twenty years, but he still can't remember that the closet light shines right into her eyes, so he turns it on. She makes him aware of his error…uh, yeah, so he closes the closet door quickly. If you've ever tried to close a door quickly, you know where the phrase "slam the door" comes from. It actually comes from a Latin word… just kidding. So now he's in the closet with the light on and the door closed and should be doing fine, except that only one shoe is in the closet and his socks are in the nightstand drawer way over on his side past the dresser and the toe-eating bed frame.

This is why some bait stores also sell shoes and socks and occasionally a pair of pants.

CHAPTER 4-- FISHING PART 2

I want to continue my fish story, since I only got as far as getting dressed in the last part. While I was waiting for Clyde to pick me up, I thought about why I was up so early. As I thought about it, I realized I didn't have to work and I could have slept in. There are many reasons why men fish; some I cannot share because we don't want the women to know. But I think it would be an interesting study. Maybe someone looking for a doctoral thesis in psychology should check into it. It sounds like a book deal and a movie might be possible. Maybe you could get one of the boat companies, or rod and reel firms to sponsor you...kind of a fishing grant.

Let me insert something here. I have not had a fishing license in years, if I ever had one. I used to fish with a cane pole and didn't need one for that back then. The only fishing I have done as an adult was surf fishing and someone told me I didn't need a license for that. If that's not true, I'm hoping no one with authority is reading this or the statute of limitations has expired because it was in the late seventies. So I went out on Friday and bought what they now call a "license to fish" which sounds sort of like James Bond's license to kill.

It appears they will let anybody have a license to fish if they have the money. There were no questions about my knowledge or skill level or if I had trained in terrorist camps or anything like that. They were most worried about whether I was really a resident of Florida or not. I didn't know the fish cared about that sort of thing, but I guess it could be embarrassing for a Florida fish to be caught by somebody from New York or worse yet, a Canadian, eh.

Come to find out, they only wanted to know so they could sock it to the non-residents by charging them a lot more. Well, I'm all for that. I think there should be some sort of ridiculously high toll at the Florida line that people have to pay to get in. A fee so high that it would keep most of them out…maybe $100,000 or something like that. I'm thinking we would get a lot fewer visitors; but the ones we got would be of a higher caliber than we're getting now. We'll see if they really want to come in. Some of you think we would lose too much tourist money; but the high fee would make up for the people who only come to take up room and buy a tee shirt at Ron Jon's. Maybe it would keep out those who come to pay $300,000 for a $75,000 house built out of pressed board on a piece of land the size of a '67 Chrysler.

I did notice something on the back of my license…it said if I was born after 1975, I couldn't get a hunting license without taking a course. Now that makes sense; you might need to pay someone to show you from which end of the gun the bullet exits. But if safety is such a concern for hunters, why don't they care about the safety of fishermen. I worked as a hospital chaplain for 12 years and have been in the emergency room enough to know some of the stories of how those fish hooks got there… amazing places. Somebody should have warned them about that.

I figured I knew enough about fishing to handle my license responsibly, until I picked up a little brochure next to the cash register (excuse me, next to the computer; nobody has cash registers anymore). It explained when each fish was in season and how big it had to be or how big it couldn't be for me to actually keep it. Some fish can only be caught on Thursdays which fall on an odd numbered day of the month, and only if it is between seventeen and a half inches and eighteen and a quarter inches long. You can't weigh fish anymore because some of them are embarrassed about their weight problem and that falls under some sort of cruelty to animals statute.

The clerk thought I should buy the $120 computerized calipers, which measure your fish and tell you if it is legal size for that day of the year and phase of the moon. The information for that day downloads from a satellite run by the game and fish commission. If your fish is not of legal size for that day the GPS alerts officials as to your whereabouts just in case you try to keep it anyway. I think they want everybody to just throw them back, because they've seen the professionals do that on TV and think it's cool. One pro even kisses the fish before he releases it. That's just sick.

CHAPTER 5--
FISHING CONTINUED

Sorry, last time I sort of went postal about the fishing license. Here is more of the trip.

We drove for a while, because you can't fish too close to home. I'm not sure about the reason for this and I'm not sure anyone knows the answer, but I've never gone fishing with anyone where we just walked across the street to a lake or creek that was there. Come to think of it, when I was a boy, my dad and I always drove to at least a neighboring town or maybe even another state. I think it has something to do with passing a place where you can stop and have breakfast. A part of early morning fishing is having breakfast; and since I am probably one of only three men in Florida whose wife would be willing to get up and make breakfast, everybody else usually stops. This sometimes involves a little greasy place like Waffle House. Just so you know, I love the Waffle House, and the greasy comment is an affectionate term, not criticism. There are usually other guys eating who are also going fishing, and maybe a truck driver or two, and a cop. Who else gets up at this time on a Saturday?

Instead of a good, greasy place, we stopped at a McDonald's drive-thru, which must be the new way to do the breakfast thing. I have not been fishing in years, so I'm guessing this is one more time-honored tradition that has been lost in this new society of ours. I'm sure this culture change came about because McDonald's probably sponsors one of those fishing shows on TV or advertises in the fishing magazines with a picture of some national bass tournament winner eating a McGriddle.

Who names this stuff? In my humble opinion, the culture of fast food and big box stores will be the downfall of our country. They give us the worst food and other poor quality products, but it is cheap and convenient, so "We're lovin' it." Please forgive my foray into social commentary, this isn't the time or place for that.

While we ate breakfast in the truck, we drove to a private lake that Clyde knows about. It was owned by an old friend of his and if I knew where it was, I'd tell you, but I didn't pay attention to how we got there. It was a fairly small lake. My wife, who grew up on Lake Michigan, likes to call these things ponds. It was cleanly mowed along the edges so you didn't have to worry about snakes crawling up your pants leg while you were trying to get close enough to the water to cast. Some of you ladies didn't even know this was a problem while fishing, did you? Snakes crawling up your pants leg is a huge problem. This is why most people spend $20,000 or more for a boat, so they can get away from the shoreline where all of the snakes are waiting for some unsuspecting guy with loose pants. Let me, for the record, say, "I am not scared of snakes." Now, if one startles me, I will jump as high as the next guy, but I am not afraid of them. I must admit, though, the idea of one crawling up my pants leg, poisonous variety or not, gives me the willies. Some of you didn't even know about the tribulations we endure to go fishing.

I didn't see any snakes, but Clyde mentioned he had seen an eight-foot alligator the last time he fished there. Let me say, I'm not afraid of alligators either, but I do have a healthy respect for them. I'm convinced that whenever people are wrestling them on TV, there are several unseen marksmen with rifles; just in case the gator hasn't read the script or the drugs wear off.

As soon as we started to fish, a smaller 'gator, maybe five feet or so, came out to watch. Now, why would a young alligator want to watch two old guys fish? Maybe he was bored; it was a small pond. Or maybe he was the decoy, so his ever-diligent eight-foot mother, looking for a healthy breakfast for her son, could sneak up on us from behind or worse yet, from below the water at the edge. Didn't you see Crocodile Dundee when the croc grabbed that half-dressed woman's canteen and almost pulled her into the water? We didn't have one of those foot-long Bowie knives, so I was a bit concerned about the motive of this mini-gator.

Let me note here, that a small child alligator and an eight-foot mother alligator might inspire the thought of a twelve-foot father 'gator, especially to those of us with a healthy respect. At one point the small one, which was only one of many (they have brothers and sisters, you know), started getting a little too close to shore, so Clyde decided to throw a rock at him. I thought this was a good idea since the 'gator dad would likely be mad at Clyde and eat him first, although Clyde was carrying the keys to the truck.

In the end, we caught three bass. Clyde caught two, and I caught one. Clyde's were thirteen inches, but I think mine was bigger, maybe thirteen and a half, but they have to be fourteen to keep, so we threw them back. After all, we are law-abiding citizens, and it takes at least four thirteen inchers to make a meal, anyway.

After a while, we realized the fish were all cowering on the other side because they were afraid of the alligator, so we drove to another lake, or pond. This was a beautiful spot, except for the possible snake up the leg thing, so we decided to just sit on the bank and enjoy the morning breeze and sunshine without being bothered by having to reel in any big fish. Oh, we threw out our lines just in case anyone drove by. How stupid would that look, just sitting by a pond without a line in the water? Between our wanting to just enjoy the outdoors and the fish not biting, we had time to sit and chat.

I believe that's why a lot of guys fish. It gives them time to sit with a friend and just talk. That's been lost to us guys in this modern world. How long has it been since you saw a small general store with men sitting around on the porch playing checkers and smoking a pipe? I don't think Wal-Mart even has a porch. If you're seen just sitting around talking, people, especially women, think you're loafing. If you have a fishing pole or a shotgun in your hand, it's seen differently; you're doing something. It could be a bowling ball; why else would anyone do that? We men do things just to be together as men and talk. We go to ball games, NASCAR races, motorcycle rallies (well, there women pull up their shirts, but that's not why we go), and we hunt and fish. This is important enough to us that we are willing to brave the dangers of snakes up our pants leg and alligators.

If someone would open a chain of small general stores with porches, I think you could do pretty well.

CHAPTER 6--
I BROKE MY ARM
IN THE ER

On June 1, 1996, I broke my arm while I was in the emergency room at Wuesthoff Hospital. I know you usually go to the ER after you break your arm, but not me; I went there to break it.

Well, I really didn't go there for that purpose, but that's where it happened. You see, I was the hospital chaplain and was paged in that Saturday morning at around 4:45 to be with a family of someone who had died. The death wasn't unexpected, as the girl had been seriously ill for some time, but it was still difficult for the family.

When I arrived, the family was in the room with the girl and after talking with them for awhile and having prayer, I escorted them to a small waiting room that we used for such occasions. We were leaving to give the nurses a chance to clean things up and remove some of the stuff they had used to try to save her, so she would look a little better for the family. In the hallway were little yellow signs saying to be careful because the floor was wet. Actually, it was being waxed. So we tiptoed around the signs to get into the room.

We talked about the things you talk about when someone has died and after fifteen or twenty minutes, I came out to see if the nurses were ready for the family to return. Do you remember what I just wrote regarding the wax? Well, at the moment, I didn't. I guess I was a little preoccupied with the situation and, remember, by now it's around 5:30. So I strolled out of the room, stepped into a puddle of wax and did what must have been a beautiful imitation of someone on TV stepping on a banana peel. Both feet came up to a place that I would guess was chest high and for a moment, which seemed suspended in time, I was hovering over the wax in a horizontal position. It was as if I was out of my body looking down on myself...no wait, that's a different story.

Being unable to hold that midair posture for very long, I soon headed for the floor. I stuck my hand down to break my fall and landed in the wax. Just a side note...I was wearing a brand new suit. It appeared that I had failed to break my fall but had succeeded in breaking something. My left hand seemed to be coming out of the sleeve of my coat in a fairly awkward angle, and it was very painful.

I walked into the nurses' station and calmly said, "I think I broke my arm." David Segona, who had his back to me and who has now become a RN/Paramedic on a helicopter, and who I hope has developed a greater sense of compassion, turned around and responded, "Oh, yea, big deal!" When he looked down at my wrist, his eyes got a little wide and he said, "Oh, I think you did; besides you're starting to look a little pale, and let's get you something for pain." I thought that was a good idea and my opinion of him improved greatly. He reached out to grab me as pale headed toward faint and I was considering returning to the floor. He walked me to a room and got me onto a stretcher.

By this time the rest of the night staff came in to see what was going on. I felt comforted, these were my friends. I had been their chaplain for three years and had spent a lot of time in the ER with them through some pretty difficult stuff. So, they started making fun of me for falling. Isn't it nice to have friends?

When they were done and the fun was over, Curtis Gray, our paramedic, took out those big scissors they carry and prepared to cut the sleeve of my coat. They just love cutting peoples' clothes off. I'm not sure why! I politely informed him that the suit was new and I had no intention of letting him cut my coat off. I felt like Clint Eastwood in Dirty Harry; remember that ER scene? Anyway, the jacket would easily slip off my arm...that was new to Curtis and he reluctantly holstered his weapon.

By this time, the doctor had been made aware of the VIP patient and had taken note of the angle of my wrist and had ordered an x-ray and, thank God, a pain shot. Fortunately our nurse who called herself "Bonnie Drop Your Drawers" worked dayshift, and would not be available to give me my shot in the butt. I think it was David, who was still feeling bad about his "big deal" comment, who kindly administered the pain medication in my arm.

Things are starting to get a little fuzzy…I'll have to finish this later.

CHAPTER 7--
I BROKE MY ARM IN
THE ER--PART 2

In Part 1, I failed to mention the name of the ER doctor who took care of me that morning before the surgeon was called. It was Col. George Martin. He was our only African-American physician and he didn't get to work with us very often. He was a great doc and really fun to work with. He was an Air Force flight surgeon and had connections at the Space Center. He had hoped to be an astronaut, but it never happened. A few years later, he was killed in a airplane crash during a mission on Guam. If you're interested in reading about it, here's a link to that story: http://www.cnn.com/2008/WORLD/asiapcf/07/23/guam.b52.crash/. They were going to do a fly over for Guam's Liberation Day celebration. My dad and I went to Guam for that one year, because my dad was one of their liberators, but that's another story!

I also forgot to mention that right before I passed out from the pain shot, Katie Scholl, one of our nurses leaned down and whispered something in my ear. She told me which orthopedic surgeon was on call that night and that I didn't want him. She said, "When Dr. Martin asks you if you have a preference, tell him Larry Robinson." I was able to mumble it out right before I went to sleep.

Well, by the time I woke up, the day shift crew was starting to come in, so a whole new group of friends had their chance to make fun of me. The surgeon was there, as was my wife and son. I noticed that I had a cast on from my hand up to my arm pit. I was still really groggy, so I didn't pay much attention to it. The surgeon was telling me that he really thought I would have to have surgery, but he hoped the cast would work. An x-ray on Monday would let us know.

They discharged me before I was really awake. I don't even remember leaving the hospital, but I woke up in the car as we were sitting in the McDonald's drive through, getting something for my son, Scott. I freaked out when I realized I had a cast up to my arm pit. I told Kathy to head back to the ER.

Maybe I've not mentioned before about my claustrophobia…well that includes casts. I had a cast on my wrist once and took it off in the middle of the night with a screwdriver. That was after I tried a Valium. Maybe I didn't give it long enough. I once had a cast on my lower leg that I cut down the back until I could slip it off and on like a cowboy boot. This was before the days of those Velcro boots they have now.

Anyway, when I returned to the ER, I told them to call the surgeon back to get this cast off, now. Where's "Bonnie Drop Your Drawers" when you need her? I needed another shot and the butt would have been fine with me. If you think they made fun of me before, well, this was a whole new level of fun now, with me freaking out. The surgeon came down and when I told him he had to get it down below my elbow, he said he couldn't do that and still immobilize the wrist. So he cut it off just above the elbow so it didn't go up very far and then split it on the top and the bottom the full length of the cast and wrapped it. So, basically, my cast had the strength of an ace bandage, but I knew I could take it off easily if I needed to. The surgeon sent me home with more Valium…he thought it might help. It did this time! I'm thinking he gave up on the idea of the cast working at all.

The x-ray on Monday showed that I needed surgery. Duh! After surgery, I woke up with an external fixator. It was a big metal thing hooked to screws that went into the bone and were coming out through the skin. It looked like a television antenna, but was better than a cast. You can Google "external fixator" and see pictures of one.

The interesting thing about it was that if I stood near a TV, it picked up the Playboy channel.

CHAPTER 8-- JOHNNY CASH

Johnny Cash died September 12, 2003. He was an amazing man. He went through some terrible and wonderful times. He, or one of his friends at the time, said, "Never get your pills mixed up with your spare change; I did that once and swallowed 85 cents." I think that must have been during the terrible times. He later found his way back to his roots and became a man of deep faith, influencing many in the music industry.

It is interesting to see how people change as they get older. Some people sow their wild oats while they are young and then gradually mellow. Others never really get a chance to sow those oats while young because of their own motivation for school, or a job, or simply out of respect for (or fear of) their parents. Sometimes these people end up trying the wild side later in life. This is usually more damaging because they now have a family of their own that can be destroyed by their bad choices.

It seems like all of us *need* a time to find out who we *really* are. A part of that is the chance to *be* someone different than us. After spending some time being different, we usually come back to who we were to start with. In other words, we return to our roots. Proverbs 22:6 says, "Train up a child in the way he should go and when he is old, he will not depart from it." It doesn't say they will never leave it, but says they will return. Many parents have struggled throughout their lives waiting to see their children return to the values they were taught. Unfortunately, the parents often die before they see that return. Sometimes the death of a parent *is* the catalyst that brings the emotional turmoil leading back to the roots of faith. For many, though, by the time they decide to get back to who they were, there have been huge changes brought on by the consequences of their choices. The person they hoped to get back to is forever changed.

I'm listening to Johnny Cash as I write. He is singing, "Sunday Morning Coming Down" which was written by Kris Kristofferson, another well-known oat-sower of the wild variety. It begins with these words:

"Well, I woke up Sunday morning with no way to hold my head that didn't hurt. And the beer I had for breakfast wasn't bad so I had one more for dessert. Then I fumbled in my closet through my clothes and found my cleanest dirty shirt. Then I washed my face and combed my hair and stumbled down the stairs to meet the day."

What a picture of a man looking for who he really is and not liking who he finds, and feeling unable to get back to who he was. The song goes on...

"Then I walked across the street and caught the Sunday smell of someone's frying chicken and Lord it took me back to something that I lost somewhere, somehow along the way."

Here's the chorus, all together now:

"On a Sunday morning sidewalk, I'm wishing Lord that I was stoned. 'Cause there's something in a Sunday that makes a body feel alone. And there's nothing short of dying, that's half as lonesome as the sound of the sleeping city sidewalk and Sunday morning coming down."[1]

Even if we've never been in that exact place, most of us can relate to the feeling of loneliness that is found in a place without our roots. When the Sunday you grew up with is no longer a day rooted in worship and fellowship, it is hard to get through it.

By the way, I hope you find yourself...and I hope you like who you find. If not, you have to live with the person you've become in the searching. May God grant us the grace for that, because we'll surely need it!

---

1   Kris Kristofferson 1969, "Sunday Mornin' Comin' Down".Sunday Morning Coming Down, Johnny Cash, Columbia Records, 1972.

CHAPTER 9--
TIME

For a short period of my life, before I knew better, I worked as a police officer while we were waiting on grant money so I could just be a chaplain. Those three years were eye opening to a naïve young pastor. It was a side of life that I had never experienced.

The most interesting part of the job was midnight shift. We worked a seven day rotating shift; so each month we started with seven evenings, then one day off followed by seven days; then two days off, but at eleven o'clock on the second night off, you had to go in for your first of seven midnights. This meant you had to sleep some of your second day off to get ready for midnights; then seven midnights in a row before the long awaited four day weekend. I almost got an ulcer from that schedule.

That first midnight, without any rest, you start getting sleepy around one o'clock in the morning. The trick now is to figure out a way to stay awake and not wreck your patrol car while driving slowly behind buildings checking for open doors or anything else suspicious. You look for anything to get your adrenaline pumping. Sometimes the things that got it pumping were funny, but only when you look back at them.

I remember one night when I was patrolling slowly around the corner of a new building in town. Suddenly, I heard something hit the side of my car and startled, I turned to see what it could be. I was then hit in the face by a large stream of water from a powerful sprinkler. We always rode with the window down so we could hear any suspicious noises. What a mistake this time! I finally realized I was not being attacked by some sort of crazed criminal with a super soaker, but I had to check to see if it was the water that had wet my car seat or if I had peed on myself. I'm pretty sure it was the sprinkler.

The only thing good about that incident is that it allowed me to drench Tina one night. Tina Papitto was a dispatcher on another shift, who hoped to become a police officer, so she rode with me sometimes for some experience (yea, good luck with that). I drove behind that building one night when she was with me and timed it just right with the sprinkler on her side of the car. I wet her real good, but it was the last time I was ever able to catch her off guard. She learned fast; she was always watching for sprinklers. There's some experience for you.

Another night, I was patrolling around a Goodyear Tire Store that was notorious for false alarms. We always had to go there in the middle of the night for an alarm. The owner even quit showing up. He would tell the dispatcher to have us check the doors and wait for the alarm to reset. Boy, come to think of it, we sure were nice. Well, this night there was no alarm, but as I was patrolling the building our sergeant came on the radio and told us to stop and write down information concerning a BOLO. That's cop talk for a vehicle to "be on the lookout" for. I stopped before exiting the parking lot and took out my clipboard and laid it against the steering wheel so I could write. I turned on the overhead light, which we hated to do because it makes you so visible and vulnerable sitting inside the car. Suddenly there was a blaring car horn, and again startled (a recurring theme), I slammed my car into gear and floored it. As I exited the parking lot onto the street (rather rapidly as I remember), I turned sharply and hit the brakes so I could skid around to face whoever was blowing their horn (don't get ahead of me here). To my surprise, there was no one there; no cars, nothing. I sat for a moment wondering where in the world the horn…wait a minute, I slowly tried my own horn. Yep, same sound. With the clipboard on the steering wheel I had managed to nearly scare the poop out of myself. You had already figured that out, hadn't you? Well, you had to be there.

One more…Tina was with me again, and we received a burglary call from a house in her neighborhood. We arrived at the house and parked in front. When we went inside, we were informed that it appeared nothing had been touched but that when they came in, they thought they saw someone run out through their backyard. We walked out back and saw a car driving away on the next street behind them. Tina and I ran for the car, jumped in and I started backing down the street really fast. Any of you who have tried to drive really fast backwards know what happened. The car began to swerve a little from side to side and suddenly did a perfect J-turn and spun around (coming frighteningly near a telephone pole) and ended up facing the direction I wanted to go. I put it in drive and drove to the stop sign. The car we were chasing had turned and came past us at the intersection. Tina said, "Oh, they're neighbors, they live on that street." So I slowly turned right and drove through the neighborhood trying to keep my trembling right leg from being obvious to Tina. After a few quiet moments, she finally asked, "Did you mean to do that?" You'll have to find Tina to get the answer. You should also ask her about Marty Robbins and "El Paso."

I called this chapter Time. The reason for that is midnight shift has a peculiar time warp, an odd combination of boredom and excitement (even if we cause it ourselves). I wrote a poem about it, but as Archie Bunker would say, "It doesn't even rhyme."

MIDNIGHTS

Time, seconds slowly tick away to become
the minutes and hours of the night.
Seconds which keep rhythm with a quietly
beating heart as you patrol,
Fighting the boredom of monotonous streets
and buildings and people,
Wrestling to keep your mind on the job;
driving and dreaming.
Seconds, dragging their way to a much needed
cup of coffee, a conversation with anyone.

Time, seconds racing to keep up with a
pounding heart.
The call - lights and sirens seem godlike
as they exert their control over time.
Seconds, moving ever so quickly to
consume valuable minutes,
Once useless divisions of an hour, now precious;

once abundant, now fleeting.
It's over--"unit clear."

The racing hands of the clock stop abruptly and
again begin their monotonous movement.
And your heart listens to find the rhythm
of the ticking of time.

CHAPTER 10-- ROOFING

I went to my sister's in Georgia for Thanksgiving. My mom and dad were going to be there and the 24th is also my mother's birthday. It was one of those milestones of age that we won't mention. She wasn't expecting me to come, so it was a neat surprise for her. But the greatest surprise was mine. My sister and brother-in-law have built an addition onto the back of their house...a big addition. It almost doubles the size of their home. They told me about it on the phone and I thought it was a wonderful thing for them. Rick has become a pretty good "handyman" down through the years and with help from some friends and a few professionals from church, they got the addition ready for shingles. There was a roofer from their church who was going to do the job for them, but before he could get to it, he broke his ankle. Take a moment and see if you can guess where this is going.

So, here we are on Thanksgiving morning, carrying eighty pound bundles of shingles up a ladder onto the roof. Surprise!! Did you guess it? After two trips up the ladder, Rick, who's my age, and I quickly developed a system so that the two younger guys (his sons-in-law) climbed the ladder and handed off the shingles to us. We still had to walk up an angled roof and across the house to place the bundles, but it was better than the ladder. I could only imagine the pain I would feel in my legs the next day. We finished getting them up and stopped before the meal was served. It was a great Thanksgiving together as family. I was most thankful that all the shingles were up on the roof and we had the afternoon off.

HERB AGEE

Unfortunately, it takes me a couple of days to feel the pain of soreness. I've always been that way. Sometimes I can't even remember what I did a couple of days ago that's making me hurt so much today. The result was that I felt okay the next day and agreed to go up on the roof to help lay the shingles. We had two two-man crews going and I was laying the shingles and Brian would nail them with the nail gun. My job involved squatting down to lay the shingle in place on the chalk line and then getting up to get another shingle and squatting down to lay it in place. If you can imagine doing this all day, squatting, standing, squatting, standing; by late afternoon my legs felt like noodles. It was all I could do to stand up and walk around. Thank God for sunset.

We finally had to quit before it got so dark that we might walk off the edge of the roof. I barely noodled down the ladder. I was already planning to leave the next day, but decided to go early enough that there would be no expectation of my helping anymore. I was still weak in the legs, but was not too sore yet. I drove home on Saturday which meant that the "soreness" would manifest itself on Sunday morning. Oh, joy!

I awoke Sunday morning to strange noises. It sounded like someone was dying in my bedroom. After a moment I realized that the sound was coming from me. I was moaning. It hurt just to move. Crawling out of bed was unbearable. I stumbled into the kitchen and took a handful of ibuprofen. My kidneys would have to fend for themselves. My legs were so sore that it was agony just to lift them to walk. Taking a shower and trying to dress was like being tortured. You know how singing in the shower gives that fullness to your voice? It does the same with moaning and groaning. I dropped the soap and just looked at it. It would be okay down there. Bending over to put on my socks and shoes hurt so badly that I considered going barefoot.

I made it to church, but I was wishing for a healing service instead of one for worship, but I wouldn't have known where to tell them to anoint, everything hurt. As we began the processional hymn, I looked at the steps up to the platform and wondered if I would ever make it up. I had never noticed how many steps there were or how high they looked. Six huge steps…how did they expect people to get up these things? A chair lift for the handicapped would have come in real handy. As I climbed, I was moaning at each step. I moaned sitting down and moaned standing up. I didn't realize I was moaning out loud until Pastor Dave whispered, "What's wrong with you?" I leaned over, "Tell you later, ooohhh!" I shouldn't have done that.

I sure hope they're finished with the house by Christmas.

CHAPTER 11—
MY WIFE IS AWAY

Candy left today to go to Orlando to spend some time with her daughter. Any man knows that when his wife leaves, things are going to be weird. We're always kind of glad they're leaving at first because it gives us time to ourselves. It is a time for fantasy...oh, not the kind you're thinking of. We fantasize that while she's gone, we will have some time to do a lot of things we need to do that we can never get done when she is here. We're not sure why we can't get them done while she is home, and we're never really exactly sure what it is we need to do, but we feel like we can find it and get it done while she's gone.

Then, we come home from work and she's not there. Suddenly, we have no idea what it was we were going to do, or any inclination to even look for what it was. We don't feel like doing anything. We begin to mope. I'm not sure exactly what that word means; mope, but I have surely experienced it. Actually, I'm experiencing it now.

We look for something to eat. We eat things she meant to throw out before she left, but since it's there, we risk eating it. It might kill us, but we don't really care; we're lonely and feel like we might die anyway. We watch stuff on TV we never usually watch and we don't particularly enjoy, but it takes up time. By the way, they have a special channel for everything now. Believe me, you can spend the biggest part of an evening just flipping through the channels and spending enough time on each one to figure out what its specialty is.

We drive around looking for something to do or someplace to go or someone to be with so we can fill the time while she's gone.

Unfortunately, most of our friends are married, too, and their wives are home, so we don't have anybody to hang out with. Those guys lucky enough to still have single friends can call to see what exciting things they are doing and "can we join them?" Married men think single guys are always doing exciting stuff. You find out they are just sitting at home watching one of those weird TV channels... so much for the exciting life.

The best part of the evening is when she calls to say goodnight. For a few minutes, all is right with the world again. Unfortunately, she usually remembers some stuff that needed to get done while she was gone and asks if you did it. So now, after wasting the whole evening, you end up in the garage or the yard or under the sink or in the shed or in the attic doing something that was sort of in the back of your mind all along, but you really didn't want to get around to doing and hoped she wouldn't ask about.

That's why the single guy is watching TV; he doesn't have someone he loves enough to do this stuff for. But he's lonely all the time, and we only have to endure it occasionally.

Honey, please hurry home.

CHAPTER 12--
NEW YEAR

Oh, wow, we're starting on the backside of this decade. What happened to the 50's and 60's? And the 70's, 80's and 90's? Just when I get accustomed to a decade, it moves on. I even had to cope with changing millennium a few years ago. I guess I finally need to admit and come to grips with my personal issues about change. I've decided I don't particularly like change. I don't see why people move to a bigger house or remodel bathrooms. I don't even see any reason to buy new furniture unless what you have is worn out and then I think you should try to find something that looks and feels just like what you had. People used to die in the same house where they were born, for Pete's sake.

Change does bring about some funny stuff, though. A good friend of mine recently took out his checkbook to pay for something, and a snotty-nose little kid (they're all snotty-nose, you know) working behind the counter said, "A check? Get with the times, man." Now, that was funny, but can you believe it? Checks are so last millennium, I guess. And then, this same friend was at a meeting of his profession (I'm trying to keep Pastor Dave's identity a secret, so as not to embarrass him) and a fellow professional made fun of his cell phone because it only makes phone calls (he's since upgraded). The new ones take pictures and videos and download music and movies and do things you don't even want to know about, like telling the government where you are at all times through the GPS chips. I'm kidding about that last part. I hope. The fact is cell phones have become so technical that it's hard to figure out how to just make a call. I have been looking for a cell phone with a rotary dial, but it seems no one makes those. If any snotty-nose kid writes back and asks, "What's a rotary dial?" You're done for.

It seems that everyone wants the newest, the latest, the greatest of everything. I remember the phone in our hallway that lasted through my whole childhood. There was no reason to change; a new phone looked just like the old one, black. I miss that. My grandmother's phone number started with TH7 and the phone weighed 40 pounds. Now, that's a phone...and a weapon. Today, people wear phones in their ears like hearing aids. You can't whack a burglar with one of those.

I hope my next big change is to the "other" side of life. Just so you know...Heaven is "old-fashioned." It's the other place with all the technology.

CHAPTER 13-- NO HOCKEY TONIGHT

Well, it has happened again. Cable TV has failed me. No, it's still working, there's just no hockey game on tonight. There should be a hockey game on some channel every night, at least during hockey season. I'm sure there was a hockey game played somewhere tonight, but I couldn't watch it.

Where we lived in Orlando, there was no cable, yet. We were pretty rural. We had an antenna, but there's very little hockey on network TV. We could have gotten a dish, but we really didn't have time to watch much TV. We watched sunsets instead. Here, we have cable and a little more time to watch since I don't drive forty-five minutes to work once or twice (if paged back in) a day. Have I mentioned that I drive forty-five seconds to work now, and that's taking the long way?

Growing up in South Carolina did not develop much of a love of hockey for me. Ice wasn't very abundant and I never even saw hockey unless it was during the winter Olympics and then I could never understand the rules; offside, icing and worst of all, in Olympic hockey, they don't fight. Oh, I know, you don't watch it for the fights. Yeah, really? Don't ever believe the fans who say they don't enjoy the fights; they're lying. They watch NASCAR for the wrecks, too. I even watch Wheel of Fortune and hope somebody will fall over the counter when they lean way out to spin the wheel. It needs "something" exciting. Maybe it's just me. Anyway, I never really cared for hockey until my son, Scott, started playing when he was about ten or eleven years old. By being at every practice and game, I finally understood the rules and eleven year old kids skate and play at a slower pace which allowed me to get used to following the puck. Before that, I never knew where it was after it was dropped on the ice.

Well, I fell in love with the game, except for the time Scott was checked so hard that he blew snot all over the inside of his face mask. Yuck! But that aside, learning hockey even helped me understand soccer, which, I think, is hockey on a big field without the ice and the skates, and the stick is your feet and the puck is a ball. Those last two items are why soccer players have more teeth than hockey players, besides the fact that they fight less. By the way, I have not learned to love soccer and I apologize to the European hooligans who act like the sun rises and sets in soccer.

But this is about hockey on TV. Now, I realize I live in Florida where hockey has not had a great following. My wife grew up in the upper peninsula of Michigan on the Canadian border and hockey was about the only thing they could get on TV and radio. But, experts say that our area is full of snowbirds from Michigan and Canada. They love hockey! Wouldn't you think the TV stations and advertisers would want to target this market? But no, I sit down with plans to watch a good hockey game, maybe even the Tampa Bay Lightning... and nothing. There was plenty of junk on and even some good shows. There was a special on Johnny Cash, and you know how I feel about him, but it wasn't hockey.

I mean, come on, there is a channel just for food and cooking, one just for home and garden stuff (by the way, I think that's the devil's channel, but more about that later), several specialty channels for various types of music, one for history, one for game shows (as if there weren't enough game shows on regular TV). There's comedy, travel, racing, all kinds of sports (poker's a sport?). I even once saw a Scrabble match on ESPN (you've got to be kidding), and C-Span lets you watch the government at work (Whoopee!); and believe it or not, there is a channel that features weather twenty-four hours a day, as if you can't go outside and see that.

How about a hockey channel on my basic cable system, huh?

CHAPTER 14--
HOME AND GARDEN
CHANNEL

When I wrote about no hockey the other night, I mentioned the Home and Garden channel. I made the off-hand remark that I thought it was of the devil. There is a reason for my understanding.

First, let's look at the food channel. Here is a channel where a woman (or man) can watch a professional chef prepare a gourmet meal, write down the ingredients and instructions and then give it a try. Now, if said woman (or man) lives alone or is already a proficient cook, this is okay. This way, either the novice cook gets to eat the experiment themselves, or the proficient cook is able to make a wonderful meal for themselves and the family. But what happens when the cook is not proficient and there is a family they are cooking for? You know what happens. They are fed a concoction of gourmet items in a fashion that cannot be recognized and with a taste nowhere near the promised delicacy implied on TV.

Professionals on TV are able to make everything look easy, that's why they are called professionals. Duh. They take a little paring knife (that you can buy for three easy payments) and with a couple of potatoes, a radish, three lemons, and an apple, they make a delightful little nativity scene complete with an angel and a donkey. It looks so easy. But once you get the knife and try your luck, you simply end up with some vegetables and fruit that look like they were part of a grotesque experiment by a serial killer. Not only are the carvings "not too good," but they are spattered in your blood because the only honest part of the commercial was, "This knife is way sharp; we are professionals, do not try this at home without paramedics standing by." You didn't notice this because it was said very rapidly in a voice that only dogs and lawyers can hear. So now you not only have three easy payments that aren't as easy as you thought, but you have an emergency room bill, ER doctor bill, an ambulance bill (some friend…afraid you will bleed in his new car), and a penalty fee because the ER was not in your insurance network.

But this started out about H&G. Let me explain why I think the Home and Garden channel is of the devil. I give this commentary as one who is "handyman challenged." I remember once when my first wife, Kathy, answered the phone and someone asked, "Is Herb handy?" She replied, "No, but he's standing right here." She thought that was so funny. I guess it was, except for the fact that the truth is seldom funny.

Let me take a moment here to advise any man who can't fix squat to never marry a woman whose father is a handyman. She not only comes with all the emotional baggage of every woman, but she thinks that husbands can fix anything. So on the honeymoon, she expects you to repair the lamp by the bed in the hotel room that won't work, because "daddy always carried tools with him for just this kind of thing." Not only will you never be able to impress your wife, but your father-in-law will think you're, shall we say, less than a man.

Now, with that said, you can imagine someone who is handyman challenged finding that his cable system has the Home and Garden channel. This demonic place is filled twenty-four hours a day with projects that he cannot possibly do, and his wife loves to watch it. Somehow he is talked into trying a small, easy project, and it drags on from days to weeks to months, until he has to hire a real handyman to finish the job, or, God forbid, his father-in-law comes to help. This channel is a nightmare waiting to happen. With the food channel, the woman can, at least, take on the recipe by herself. The projects from H&G almost always, and I, to be politically correct, say almost, take a man (translated, husband) to do the work. Although they often show women doing the work on TV, you know guys are there off-camera to do the heavy stuff. Although some of those women look like they could…oh, never mind, I probably shouldn't go there.

The wife of a handyman challenged husband may as well watch the Science Fiction channel and expect him to beam himself down to the hardware store or watch Animal Planet and expect him to wrestle an alligator and make her a purse and shoes, as to expect him to complete a house and garden project. Channels like H&G are just setting us up for failure, and we can do that well enough on our own, thank you.

Thank goodness the cable sex channels cost too much.

CHAPTER 15--
9/11

September 11…who can ever forget that date? Just saying it gives me chills. It used to be just another day, but now something terrible is attached to it. I have a couple of friends whose birthdays are on 9/11. It doesn't seem fair their birthday is forever tied to that tragedy.

I'm sorry, but I can't think of anything light or funny to write about this day. Maybe it will change over time. Come to think of it, my first wedding was on Pearl Harbor Day some thirty-three years after the fact. That's not funny, either, but it does make me realize that after some time has passed, we tend to either forget the tragedy or get accustomed to the fact of it. Having our wedding on December 7th probably would have seemed a sacrilege to a Pearl Harbor survivor, but I wasn't alive for the attack so it was not a vivid memory for me. My dad served in the war and went ashore on Guam in the first wave of the invasion. I visited Guam with him years later. The memories still lived for him. Those memories still live for the people of Guam, too. It's only been sixty-six years since their liberation and there are still people alive who remember the cruelty of the Japanese occupation. It has not been changed to be politically correct even though the Japanese own much of the island now. Some of the people of Guam who were there for the occupation left the island when the Japanese were allowed to return and start owning property.

We have July 4th as a one day picnic and day off from work to celebrate the birthday of our country, but it has been three hundred years for us. Guam has a week-long liberation celebration that involves the whole family and everyone takes off. They treated my dad like a hero and called him "one of our liberators." Even those who are second and third generation still remember the stories. It's a part of remembering their history and passing it on without revisionists correcting it..

I hope we never forget 9/11, but in some way I hope maybe my great-grandchildren will only have an historical view and not an emotional attachment to September 11.

CHAPTER 16--
UP EARLY

It's 5:45 am. Doesn't sound like a song title, does it? Do you remember the 1970's band, Chicago? Did you know that the title of their song "25 or 6 to 4" is a reference to the time of day? As Robert Lamm was writing early in the morning, he looked up at the clock and it was 25 or 26 minutes until 4:00 am. It rhymed, so why not?

Waiting for the break of day
Searching for something to say
Flashing lights against the sky
Giving up I close my eyes
Sitting cross-legged on the floor
25 or 6 to 4.

Isn't worthless trivia fun? It's amazing how much has been written during the early hours of the morning. When you awaken in the middle of the night and cannot get back to sleep because of worry or anxiety, writing seems to help settle the mind. The things that are keeping you awake are usually spinning around in your head with no real organization. It can bring on a panic feeling that you cannot explain. Writing makes you put your thoughts into words on a page or computer screen in an organized fashion.

Putting thoughts into words is a part of the value of therapy. As you talk to someone about your past or present problems or concerns, you have to make the random thoughts concrete. Sometimes just the talking helps you see the answer to your dilemma without the input of the listener.

Writing has a similar benefit. It is why therapists sometimes ask for written material. It is why Marriage Encounter and other such retreats have you write your thoughts to one another rather than just talking. It's why you see books of prayers. Writing a prayer gives it form. Have you ever tried to pray for your enemies? It's not fun. It's tough. Writing the prayer for someone who has hurt you puts you in a place where real forgiveness can start. You really know that you want good for them because it is written down. Even if you tear up a prayer or letter after you have written it, there is something cathartic or cleansing about writing it.

Oh well, it's now almost 6:30; still no song lyrics coming to mind, but at least I've made myself sleepy.

Except that I usually get up at 6:30.

CHAPTER 17-- TAXES

It's tough being honest. We've put off paying our taxes until the last possible extension date in hopes that we would have some moral lapse and be able to claim dishonest stuff to deduct. It never happened. I guess I'm glad. I can only speculate that if we had a moral lapse, we would have eventually been sorry for it and then, in a spirit of repentance and restitution, would have had to contact the IRS and let them know we had been dishonest. Then it's penalties and interest and embarrassment. Even worse, not being sorry and not contacting the IRS, but being audited and them finding the dishonesty... then comes SORRY in capital letters.

I've always questioned someone's sorrow and repentance when it comes after they got caught. Maybe I shouldn't; they probably are sorry. I guess I feel better if they get caught for something they did in the past but already quit doing; instead of getting caught in the middle and then acting so pitiful. I can buy that they are sorry they were caught; but it's hard to believe they are sorry for what they did. Maybe they are...I shouldn't judge that.

Getting caught doesn't seem to mean what it once did. Back then people lost their jobs and their reputations when they were caught. Then Clinton made it through what he shouldn't have (in my humble opinion), even though I like him. Besides, you expect the President to be smarter than that. I'm not a prude, but a church leader once told me that when he heard that a pastor had a moral lapse involving sex, he always had the church books audited, because a man who will be dishonest in his marriage relationship will be dishonest in other areas of his life. It's not always true, but it makes sense.

After Clinton, the Rev. Jesse Jackson was found to have a mistress. Not only was the press afraid to jump on that for fear of being called racist, but his own religious community, except for the few moral giants, were either afraid to speak out or seemed to accept it (sort of like Jimmy Swaggart's church did when he fell).

Nowadays, getting caught sometimes brings celebrity status instead of shame. I think we've lost shame in our modern society. I understand that shame has been used in some terrible ways through the years, but let me say, "There is still a place for shame." A child molester should be ashamed instead of feeling persecuted because people don't want them living in their neighborhood. A crooked politician should be ashamed instead of blaming everybody else. A lying, cheating CEO should be shot (I mean be ashamed) when they take the retirement income of senior citizens. A crooked developer should…oh, I'm not even allowed to put in this book what I think crooked developers should feel.

I guess most of us are glad that society has lost some of its harshness in dealing with people who fail. Failing is a terrible thing, especially moral failure. I've had some friends who have experienced it. Guys I would have put on a list of those it would never happen to. I don't like to use that word anymore -- never. I don't even use it about myself without adding hope. I hope it never happens to me. I hope it never happens to you either…there are still some really harsh people out there. I also hope you are not one of them, either.

CHAPTER 18--
VALENTINE'S DAY

Well, what do you know, it's Valentine's Day. It used to be St. Valentine's Day, but in 1969 the Roman Catholic Church dropped it from the calendar as an official feast day. You would expect that when the church dropped the day, women would have quit expecting cards or candy or flowers or jewelry on that day, wouldn't you? But no, Hallmark, Russell Stover, the florists and advertisers of fine diamonds would have none of that. Just because the Pope doesn't have a girl to buy for doesn't mean the rest of them shouldn't get something.

It is amazing how gift buying has become such a pressure. When you think about it, gifts, to be true gifts, should never be expected or demanded. When that is true, they are not gifts, but romantic extortion payments (I'm expecting a lot of wonderful responses from the ladies on this one).

I remember listening to a radio show when a couple of disc jockeys, a man and woman, were having women call in to describe their best Valentine's Day. One woman told of her first one as a newlywed. She arrived home after work and found the house dark except for scented candles lighting her way and rose petals on the path. They led to the bathroom where she opened the door to find her husband in the bubble-filled garden tub surrounded by roses and candles with a cold bottle of champagne and romantic music playing. The female disc jockey said, "Ahhhh, do you realize that all the women listening are saying, 'Why can't my husband do something like that?'" The male disc jockey asked,

"Do you want to know what all the men listeners are saying? They're saying, 'Yea, and what's he going to do next year?'"

It's sometimes true. We think the gift has to be bigger or better or more expensive or more thoughtful next year, and after a couple of years trying really hard, we just give up. While it's probably not true that it has to get better, it certainly is the feeling of society and especially of the advertisers.

I, on the other hand, have a wonderful wife who does not like obligatory giving. She doesn't just say that, she really feels that way. Our gift giving is random. You may get a birthday gift two months early or two months late. It doesn't really matter. It fits us because we are both fairly impulsive and also tend to procrastinate.

I hope you have a wonderful Valentine's Day. I get to perform a wedding today, how cool is that? I hope your gesture of love, whatever it may be, is received with love and returned.

CHAPTER 19--
NEED DIRECTIONS?

I think the new navigation systems have taken some of the fun out of traveling. It used to be an adventure to drive into a new area and find your way around; an adventure in geography, patience and human relations...make that marital relations. Men have a need to find our way. It's in our DNA. This requires at least some knowledge of geography, like knowing the four directions, or at least where the sun rises and sets. That's usually enough for us. With this primitive information, we feel we can find anyplace we need to go. All we need is the patience to realize that it might take awhile and a few tries. AND we need a wife or girlfriend who understands that DNA thing and our need to explore.

There's a huge misunderstanding about men not wanting to ask directions. We don't mind asking for directions...we just don't like our wives telling us that we should. You don't need to stop at the first sense of not knowing exactly where you are in regard to where you're going. You wait (there's that patience thing) and try a few more turns to see if you recognize something...if not, then we would stop and ask. The problem is that women, at the first hint of uncertainty, mistakenly smell fear and immediately start with the "you need to stop and ask for directions routine." Once she starts that, we are pretty certain that we don't need to and pretty determined that we won't. No, we're not stubborn; it just becomes a matter of pride.

Have you ever noticed wives somehow have the ability to think we need directions when we are in a part of town where Rambo wouldn't get out? Yes, I would like directions, too, but I hate to ask the guy with the machete. Well, the woman pushing the shopping cart might know her way around the neighborhood, but she seems to be talking to an invisible friend right now. Oh, sure, I could ask the gentleman peeing on the sidewalk, but I hate to disturb someone during such a personal moment.

You see, with a navigation system, you miss out on these experiences meant to draw you closer together as a couple. Oh, it still takes you through the worst parts of town, but...without the yelling and screaming. This lack of emotion lessens the need for an appointment with a counselor at a later time; therefore, no added closeness.

Our ancestors who traveled across the ocean or across the prairie did not have sophisticated navigation systems and they still got to where they were going, usually. Well, some of them died, but...at least they weren't lost.

CHAPTER 20-- SHOPPING

When I wrote about needing directions, I was dealing with the difference in how men and women see things. Another area where we tend to be different is when it comes to shopping. Now I realize everyone's not the same, my brother-in-law loves to shop and my sister doesn't. But for the most part, men hate shopping and women love it.

Men, usually know what they want, go into a store they know has it, pick it up, pay and leave. Women, on the other hand, usually don't know what they want; they don't even know if they want anything or not… they just know they want to shop. They figure they'll find out if they want something by looking through all of the stores in the mall.

When they do find something they want, they can't just buy it. They have to be sure there's nothing else there they might want more, or they want to be sure this is the lowest price on this particular item. The only way to find out is to go into every other store and finger through all the merchandise to check. This sometimes takes, not hours, not days, but weeks to accomplish. This will drive a man crazy.

Now, the question is, why would a man go shopping at the mall with a woman to start with? I can tell you, they're usually not married yet and he just wants to be with her and show her how considerate he is. It's the same reason she watches football or hockey or NASCAR with him. He's not trying to be dishonest or false in this. He really does enjoy her company and thinks he would want to do this for the rest of his life. Men garden, go to art galleries, Yanni or Michael Bolton concerts and we enjoy them because we are with the woman we love. After we're married, we get plenty of together time, so where it happens becomes more of an issue. When it can be in our own living room or bedroom, strolling through the mall and touching all of the clothes loses its appeal.

That is, of course, unless it's Victoria's Secret; now there's a store men enjoy. I had a friend once who worked security in Victoria's Secret for the Christmas season. He had to keep other men away from the dressing rooms. You can bet he never called in sick. I'm not sure why we like it so much; you can't really touch the merchandise without feeling and looking like some kind of pervert. There's just something about being in the middle of all that lingerie. I don't know…but you guys understand.

Where was I? Oh yeah, shopping. Men usually don't buy new clothes until our wives or girlfriends tell us they won't be seen in public with us again until we buy a new pair of jeans, or a shirt, or shoes. A friend of mine on Facebook recently confessed she was cleaning out her closet and throwing away clothes that still had the tags on them. Now, that's a problem. I've never known a guy to do that. Oh, I've seen guys wearing clothes with the tags still on, but they just forgot to remove them and didn't know they were there. But to buy something and never wear it; that only happens with clothes that someone else buys us that we wouldn't be caught dead in. Men would never buy stuff and not wear it. That's just a woman thing!

Men, on the other hand, will buy two or three of the same thing because we like it and we don't worry about wearing it a few days in a row. Who notices what people wear anyway?

Oh yeah, women. Do they ever…

CHAPTER 21--
FLYING

I've had to fly a couple of times recently. I don't like to fly, but I flew to Ohio to perform funeral services for a church member who had been severely injured years ago as a Marine. What a privilege to be able to honor him and his family. That was worth it! Then I flew to Houston, Texas with my wife so she wouldn't have to fly alone to a hospice conference at M.D. Anderson and go to an empty hotel room every night. That was worth it too, because I'm a wonderful husband… at least that's what she says, but she exaggerates sometimes.

I don't remember the last time I flew before that. Did I mention I really don't like to fly? It's not the flying, or the landing, or even the possibility of crashing; it's being stuck in those little bitty seats with no way to get out of the plane. Yep, claustrophobia! Now, you know. First class would be better, I guess, if I could afford it, but I'm still stuck in a plane, even if the seat is bigger with more leg room and free beverages, and I feel more important than all those regular people sitting in the back.

Unless first class comes with a parachute and a door opener, it really hasn't helped me much, except for the beverages. God forbid you have to go to the bathroom. I lived on a 27 foot sailboat for two years and my head (that's boat talk for the bathroom) was a palace compared to airline bathrooms. I surely don't see how women use them…women are used to bathrooms the size of a small gymnasium, with couches and makeup tables, tanning booths and massages. That's why they're gone so long and why they go in bunches. They tell us there was a long line, but we know the real reason it takes forever.

I also hate having to get to the airport two hours early just to sit around waiting, but doesn't everyone hate that? Driving two hours to the airport and waiting for two hours would be four hours down the road in a car. Add to that the flying time and getting your luggage and renting a car and whatever time the flight's behind schedule and you have six to eight hours invested. If the trip is six to ten hours driving, I'd rather drive.

Of course, the other annoyance is security… not that I disagree with the concept. I just think we spend an enormous amount of money for what looks like a pretty unmotivated group of people doing that job. Most of them look like they might have been school bus drivers before they hired on with TSA. Not that there's anything wrong with school bus drivers; I was one, once or twice…took out a fire hydrant in an ice storm, but that's another story.

Anyway, Mr. President, here's my idea for airport security. The Army should develop another "Special Forces" whose purpose is just to protect our airports and planes. They would be glad to know that they're not going overseas to war, but they would be specially trained for this purpose. They dress in fatigues and carry machine guns, just to give everyone confidence in the protection…and dogs, they have to have dogs, sniffing dogs. You know the kind; they sniff out everything. Maybe they could have sniffed out the guy who stunk up the section I was sitting in.

Everyday or every few days, there would be some fake terrorist trying to get a weapon or explosive through the gates. They would have a password to say that would immediately diffuse the crisis. If the soldiers at that gate miss the fake, there would be some kind of disciplinary action, but if they caught them there would be a monetary reward. Because of the randomness of the situation, they would always be expecting something suspicious and couldn't let their guard down. I'm thinking a pretty blond, buxom girl might have a chance of sneaking something through. That's another reason for the dogs. Dogs don't get distracted by that buxom thing.

So, unless it's on a cruise ship, I don't plan to go very far from home. Well, I would consider a road trip on the motorcycle. I think maybe the openness and feeling of freedom is why I love it so much. Plus, you have wide open spaces for a bathroom…as big as the women's, just no couch.

CHAPTER 22--
FACEBOOK

Like many things in life, Facebook has its good side and bad side. Do you have a Facebook account? If not, you are really behind the Cultural Revolution. It started with MySpace and went to Twitter, but now there are dozens of social sites, as they are called. Some of them are for special interests, but many, like Facebook, are for the general public.

One of the things I love about Facebook is the opportunity to re-connect. You can list where you went to high school, college, and graduate school and find classmates with whom you have lost touch over the years. You can even find people from places where you worked in the past.

One of the things I hate about Facebook is the opportunity to re-connect. People that you really never liked can find you and ask to be your friend. They might have been the bully you dreaded seeing every day in elementary school, but now they've grown up and want to pretend that none of that ever happened. They bullied so many people, they don't even remember you. But you sure remember them! Every time your underwear rides up, you remember the many wedgies they gave you. Part of the fun of Facebook is you get to see that he's now bald and fat and looks as if he's been bullied himself by his life choices. The adult that you've become doesn't mention it, but the child in you really, really, really enjoys the pictures.

Remember the pretty cheerleader who wouldn't give you the time of day, much less go out with you? Whoa, look at her now! It's amazing what 35 years and 50 pounds can do to squash the fantasy you've carried in the back of your mind all these years. She would be playing linebacker now instead of cheering.

Then there's the plain Jane who always sat in the back of the class and few people even noticed. She has finished her career as a dancer and now does weather on TV in Las Vegas. Boy, don't you wish you had been a little nicer to her.

Actually, it's kind of fun to see where people are and where they've been. You would have never been able to guess how their lives would have turned out. But, get this...you wouldn't have been able to guess yours either. You don't even have any idea where it's going from here. It's amazing to look back and see how the hand of time or the hand of God has worked in the victories and successes and in the losses and failures to bring us to the place we are. It's funny how things work out.

Anyway, you might try Facebook. Sometimes you make a connection that becomes a real friendship...maybe even with the bully. Just let it go...he was twelve!

By the way...I only look this old because of the gray beard.

CHAPTER 23-- CHRISTMAS

'm not a big fan of Christmas…there, I said it, even though it's not a popular opinion, or at least one most often left unspoken.

Now, why would I start an article about Christmas on such a down note, when I'm such an up guy? I'm writing for all of the people who feel like me, but instead of being okay with it, they wonder what's wrong. I can tell you, nothing's wrong. There are a lot of people who not only don't enjoy Christmas; they hate the thought of it coming. It depresses them.

For many people, Christmas has bad memories attached to it. Childhood Christmas was not so great for everyone. Let me stop here to ease your mind; my Christmas memories are fine, as are my other childhood memories. Actually, it's my adult memories that give me trouble, at least the ones I can still remember.

Also, people often struggle with a special kind of grief during the holidays. Memories of holidays are more intense than regular memories, and Christmas may be filled with wonderful memories of those we've lost. We don't know how to deal with that, so instead of finding some way of honoring that person and remembering on purpose, we try to find ways of avoiding the memory. That doesn't work! So let me encourage you to make a special effort this year to remember. Put their picture in a special place; maybe light a candle at meals or at a certain time of day to represent their presence that is still alive in the memories. Talk about them to people who remember and care and will listen.

Then, there are a lot of women who dread Christmas because of the special stress it puts on them. They feel compelled to decorate and cook; maybe throw a party, and they're usually the ones who end up having to decide what to buy for everybody…whoa…I felt a sudden surge of anxiety in the force when I wrote those words, "buy for everybody."

Maybe, just maybe, there is something within us that struggles with the concept that buying expresses love. How many children would rather have a compliment from their parent instead of another toy? How many husbands or wives would prefer a word or effort of love from their spouse instead of a gift? Would someone like to spend a little time with you instead of getting some useless knick-knack? I think some of us struggle with Christmas because it is all out of whack. How did baby Jesus getting gifts from the Magi turn into a credit card nightmare?

You know, one year we decided not to buy a lot of gifts. We only bought for the children. Do you know how we felt? Guilty! Yeah, as if we had let people down or somehow not fulfilled our role in the big box store's efforts to rule the world. It was an interesting emotion, but sometimes we feel guilty when we shouldn't. I think that was one of those times. I'm guessing most people were really relieved. Maybe it took some pressure off of them, too.

I want to approach Christmas with the awe and reverence it deserves, instead of with pressure and anxiety. Maybe our giving could be to someone who really needs it, instead of more clutter for our friends and family. Check out Heifer International or the Salvation Army.

Anyway, if you are one of the people I've been talking about, let me know and maybe we can start a support group. Could one of you ladies bake some Christmas cookies to bring to the meeting? Just kidding…

Oh, yeah…Merry Christmas!

CHAPTER 24--
GOD'S HOUSE

The church's Praise Team was practicing one Tuesday night. Several adult members were away and the sound guy was gone, too, so we were practicing casually while sitting in the choir loft. The youth had been together with the youth minister all afternoon, so they were wound-up so to speak. They were laughing and having fun while we practiced. Todd Baird and I enjoyed watching them enjoy themselves. We're kind of like kids ourselves...sometimes...okay, we're old.

Anyway, as we ended practice and everyone was still talking, Ria said, "Let's pray." We always end practice with prayer, so our director, Amanda said, "Go ahead," and while everyone was still talking and laughing, Ria started praying. "God," she began, "Thank you for letting us be ourselves in your house." I was stunned! It almost took my breath away. What an amazing prayer! "Wow," I thought. Think about it. How many adult church members don't feel like they can be themselves in God's house? How many people don't come to church because they don't think they can be themselves in God's house? Somehow, we've gotten the idea that we have to be a holier version of ourselves to go inside God's house. It's why people joke about the roof falling in if they go to church.

Where did this idea come from, anyway? You guessed it, right from church people. These are the same people who sit in committee after committee talking about why nobody comes to their church and wondering how they can get more people to attend. These are the same ones who look down their noses at anyone who attends dressed differently from everybody else; who whisper to each other about how someone looks, but won't walk over to a new person to welcome them to God's house. It's like they think it's their house and they get to decide how everyone should dress and look and act. Folks, remember what we call the church? God's house! This is the same God, who, in Jesus, was accused of being a glutton and a drunkard and being a friend of and eating with sinners. Have you ever been accused of that? Has your church ever been accused of being the kind of place that sinners hang out? Then maybe you don't really consider it God's house. Maybe you consider it your house.

As I think back on that evening, I can imagine how some adults would have responded to the youth being themselves in God's house. They would have given raised eyebrows or puffs of breath intended to indicate disapproval or disgust. It's as if we always have to decide or judge someone else's method of worship. Is it appropriate or not? Based on what? Based on our understanding of worship?

This reminds me of when I was a hospital chaplain. The nurses would call me if they felt someone was not grieving appropriately. This meant they weren't grieving the way the nurse thought they should. If it was an Anglo nurse and a Jamaican, Haitian, or African-American family grieving, they would tell me to calm them down. I didn't, of course. It's how they grieve. But, if it was a German or Scandinavian family grieving, the nurse would call me to say, "They're in denial." That's translated, "They're not crying." The nurse wanted them to at least cry a little.

It seems we not only have a need for everyone to grieve the way we do, but to dress, look, worship and act in the church the way we do, or at least in a way with which we are comfortable. But, wait a minute, what did we say the church is...the house of who? God! The judging has to be left up to him. Not us!

Ok, here's the rest of the prayer. I know you were wondering...after the profound moment of thanking God for "letting us be ourselves in your house," Ria said, "and smite all of those who are laughing while I pray." I love her.

None of us got smited, by the way.

CHAPTER 25--
GIFTS AND TALENTS

The beginning of this will sound like bragging, but it's not. Hang on and you'll see.

During the last EPAS (Englewood Performing Arts Society) performance at our church, I stuck my head in the back door as I was leaving Praise Team practice. There was a six piece jazz group playing. It made me think of the many instruments I have started playing through the years.

When I was eight, I started taking piano lessons. The teacher was amazed at my ability. I soon quit. When I was in the fifth grade, I started band. I wanted to play drums (doesn't everybody?), but I was talked into the trombone. Again, the teacher was amazed at my natural talent. I quit after two years.

When I was a pastor in Lakeland, I found an old trumpet at the church and started practicing everyday in my office. I was amazed at how easy it was to get pretty good with it. Then I quit. Next, I got a great deal ($25) on a very expensive clarinet (I've always loved the clarinet) and starting learning to play. I later sold it for $400. I have played guitar on and off for years, but never long enough to be good at it. I still have two of them and a banjo, which I've never learned to play...oh, and harmonicas.

Anyway, when I looked in on the jazz group, I realized that I could be a professional musician on any of the instruments they were playing. But, I can't play any of them. Why? Because, I never developed those gifts and talents.

All of a sudden I realized that who I am, is as much about the gifts and talents I didn't develop as it is about anything else.

If I'm not careful, I can find myself feeling very guilty sometimes about all of the things I could have learned to do. But, if I had become proficient with an instrument or learned the three or four languages that I started studying, I would be a different person than I am now. I might even be in a different profession.

The fact is...we can't do everything that would have been possible for us to do. We can't be everything that we could have been. I probably haven't even done some of the stuff I should have done. But all of that is okay with me...I'm okay with who I've become. You should be okay with you, too.

You see, this is who I am. All of the good and bad that has happened in my life and all of the good and bad that I've done, or not done, is a part of me. Some of it has been blessed and some has been forgiven. This is who God and I have made together and there is no way for me to know who I could have been if I had developed other talents or made other choices.

Now, at this point of my life I can't change any of my choices from the past, but I can learn from them and continue making the good ones and maybe not continue the bad ones...maybe. And, maybe, just maybe I can still develop some gift that might be important. I doubt it, though. Most of them take some perseverance and consistency and practice... oh yeah, now I remember why I can't do any of that stuff.

CHAPTER 26--
SELLING COOKWARE

I sold cookware the first summer I was out of college. Man, it was great cookware. It was cast iron, clad in surgical stainless steel. A part of the sales pitch was showing people a study about how filthy their regular cast iron skillet was. If you test one of those, it is dirtier than a toilet. Duh, of course, it's filthy...the reason food tastes so good cooked in cast iron is that it's coated with grease from all the other meals cooked in it, and that flavors what you're cooking. The leftover grease also generates bacteria. But...guess what you do the next time you cook in it? You heat the pan. Now, I'm not a scientist or anything, but if I remember my high school biology, heat kills bacteria and germs.

They trained us to approach young single girls and offer a free gift if they would let us show them the cookware and china (yeah, some gift, a cheap set of steak knives). We would hang out at malls and wait for single-looking girls to walk by. They were usually with at least one other girl or a whole group of girls, and we had ourselves an appointment for a showing.

We had some beautiful china, too, and flatware; don't forget the knives, forks, and spoons. If we could get our foot in the door, selling was easy. Usually a girl would have a girlfriend or two with her and they would just go crazy over the stuff. It was expensive, but of course, you could pay over time.

You've probably seen it. It was "waterless" cookware. You would put something in the pan, turn it on medium just for a moment, and then turn it to low. The lid would form some sort of watertight seal and it became something like a crock pot, it could be left for hours and nothing would burn; all of the juices from the food would stay inside. One guy forgot he was cooking and went away for the weekend. He came back to a very tender roast. Some of the pans had flat lids so you could stack other pans on top of them and actually cook an entire meal on one burner, set on low, while you were at work. See, you want to buy some even now, don't you?

Back then, girls had hope chests. Some still do, but these days it's more of a plastic surgery thing. In the old days they would pack into their hope chest all of the things they would need when they got married. That's what they were hoping for, to get married. Expensive cookware that would last a lifetime surely fit the bill. Not many girls bought the china, because they expected to get that as gifts when they were married. China's always an easy choice for a wedding gift. We don't give a lot of cookware; crock pots, toasters and blenders, maybe, but not good cookware.

In those days girls still dreamed of marrying and then staying home to take care of the children and family, and that included cooking. It surely was a dream since that's the generation that saw housing go up so drastically that it took two people working to make ends meet.

I didn't do so well as a salesman, but I did sell a set of cookware to the girlfriend of Johnny Paycheck. He was the sort-of-famous country singer who sang the song, "Take This Job and Shove It." He went to prison after that. I think he shot somebody in a bar fight. We just don't have that caliber of country singer anymore. I like her singing, but I bet that never happens to Taylor Swift.

Nowadays, I'm thinking you could sell McDonald's coupons to young, single girls easier than cookware. First, this generation grew up on fast food because mom was working. Very few people cook at home anymore, and second, girls wouldn't want to admit that they expect to do most of the cooking, which owning cookware would do. They hope to have beautiful, all-wood kitchens with granite countertops from which they make…reservations.

That cooking channel may well be the salvation of cooking at home.

CHAPTER 27--
WORKING AT
PIGGLY WIGGLY

Publix is my favorite grocery store, now. Growing up in Barnwell, South Carolina, it was the Piggly Wiggly. I went shopping with my dad as a kid and started working there as soon as I turned 16. I was a pretty good bag boy and loved serving the public.

It was a small town and you became acquainted with all of the customers and learned who drove what car and on whom you could play tricks.

I usually took the groceries out before the customer had finished paying (all cars were unlocked in those days) and for many of the older ladies, I would sometimes turn their windshield wipers to fast and their radios to loud. When they finally got out to their car and turned the key, they would have a blaring radio and wipers going at full speed. It was fun to watch from the window as they would be startled and then look up to give me a friendly glare and shake their fist. People didn't give the finger much, back then.

One time, I was filling in for the produce manager and found a customer's purse open in the basket as her back was turned. I quickly grabbed a huge, double handful of pole beans and stuffed them into her purse and closed it. I listened for the moment when she was ready to pay for her groceries. As soon as she opened her purse, beans sprung out causing, first a startled scream and then a screaming of my name.

I was waiting for it, and quickly arrived to question if she was stealing produce again. I love customer service.

If you tried stuff like that today, people would probably sue the store for some kind of psychological stress. Not really, people love it when you make them feel special, and that was how they felt when they were the victims of my attention and warped sense of humor.

It's like that at our church. As the pastors ceremonially process down the aisle, I sometimes move close to the pews to elbow somebody who is sitting on the end. One woman, whose husband had been ill and later died, said he always told people about the fact that I would bump him as I came in. "It made him feel important," she said.

I don't know how you do it, but go out of your way to make somebody feel special today.

CHAPTER 28--
RIDING MY MOTORCYCLE

'm off today. It rained all night and is supposed to rain all day, too. That doesn't make much difference to most people. We need the rain and most of us have learned that you can't control the weather. We might get upset, but we usually don't take it personally. I was even supposed to do a beach wedding yesterday afternoon that had to be moved inside. When you're depending on good weather, you always have to have a plan B. But, I'm not talking about anything like a wedding or a picnic or even a day at the beach...I'm talking about riding my motorcycle. It's hard to have a plan B when you're talking about riding. It's not like you can move it indoors. Sure, you can take a car, or in my case, the van, but this isn't about getting somewhere or getting some errand done, it's about riding, just riding.

Now, for those of you who have never ridden or for those who have ridden, but don't find it the most wonderful feeling of freedom in the world, I can't explain what it means to want to ride and not be able to. The only words that would explain it are probably found in a mental health textbook...yep, I'm crazy.

Sure, I could ride in the rain, but that takes crazy to a new level. Now, any rider worth his boots will ride in the rain, but we usually get caught in it. We rarely start out in the rain, if we have another vehicle available.

Why do we love riding? I'm not sure; I just know I ride everyday. Somebody else wrote something called "Motorcycle Truth." It's all over the internet attributed to author unknown. I'll post it so you can maybe get a glimpse of my obsession.

Motorcycle Truth

A motorcycle is not just a two-wheeled car; the difference between driving a car and climbing onto a motorcycle is the difference between watching TV and actually living your life. We spend all our time sealed in boxes and cars are just the rolling boxes that shuffle us from home-box to work-box to store-box and back, the whole time, entombed in stale air, temperature regulated, sound insulated, and smelling of carpets.

On a motorcycle I know I'm alive. When I ride, even the familiar seems strange and glorious. The air has weight and substance as I push through it and its touch is as intimate as water to a swimmer. I feel the cool wells of air that pool under trees and the warm spokes of that fall through them. I can see everything in a sweeping 360 degrees, up, down and around, wider than Pana-Vision and than IMAX and unrestricted by ceiling or dashboard. Sometimes I even hear music. It's like hearing phantom telephones in the shower or false doorbells when vacuuming; the pattern-loving brain, seeking signals in the noise, raises acoustic ghosts out of the wind's roar. But on a motorcycle I hear whole songs: rock 'n roll, dark orchestras, women's voices, all hidden in the air and released by speed. At 30 miles per hour and up, smells become uncannily vivid. All the individual tree-smells and flower-smells and grass-smells flit by like chemical notes in a great plant symphony. Sometimes the smells evoke memories so strongly it's as though the past hangs invisible in the air around me, wanting only the most casual of rumbling time machines to unlock it.

A ride on a summer afternoon can border on the rapturous. The sheer volume and variety of stimuli is like a bath for my nervous system, an electrical massage for my brain, a systems check for my soul. It tears smiles out of me: a minute ago I was dour, depressed, apathetic, numb, but now, on two wheels, big, ragged, windy smiles flap against the side of my face, billowing out of me like air from a decompressing plane.

Transportation is only a secondary function. A motorcycle is a joy machine. It's a machine of wonders, a metal bird, a motorized prosthetic. It's light and dark and shiny and dirty and warm and cold lapping over each other; it's a conduit of grace, it's a catalyst for bonding the gritty and the holy. I still think of myself as a motorcycle amateur, but by now I've had a handful of bikes over half a dozen years and slept under my share of bridges. I wouldn't trade one second of either the good times or the misery. Learning to ride is one of the best things I've done.

Cars lie to us and tell us we're safe, powerful, and in control. The air-conditioning fans murmur empty assurances and whisper, "Sleep, sleep." Motorcycles tell us a more useful truth: we are small and exposed, and probably moving too fast for our own good, but that's no reason not to enjoy every minute of the ride.

CHAPTER 29-- WALKING THE DOG

Have you ever watched people walking their dog? The big question is…who's walking who? The dog is pulling on the leash, going right and left to every smell that draws their attention, while the human tries to keep their balance and not be pulled off their feet. Even tiny little dogs lead their owner around like the leash is hooked in their nose or something.

When Charley (our big red standard Poodle) was a puppy, we made the best decision we have ever made. (We don't seem to make good decisions that often). We decided to train him. The bad part was that Lucky (our six year old Cocker Spaniel) got caught up in that decision.

Candy and I were both working and Thursday was the only day we could be sure that both of us would be off. There were no obedience classes being held on a Thursday, so we went with a business that came to the house to train. That's how Lucky became a part of the situation.

When the guy came the first time, he told us that he was not there to train the dogs, but to train us. We would train the dogs. Interesting concept! He also said that dogs are pack animals and all packs have an alpha dog that leads the others. He emphasized that either we would be the alpha of the house, or one of the dogs would be.

Lucky was not happy! He could tell that trouble was coming. We had gotten Charley because we had to put Dixie down. Dixie was a wonderful German Shepherd/Doberman mix that Candy had gotten from the pound 15 or 16 years earlier. Dixie was a lady that never needed to be trained. She just seemed to know what you wanted and did it. She was the alpha and had trained Lucky as much as she could. After she was gone, Lucky became the boss, and he knew it.

The first day, the guy trained us to teach the dogs to sit and stay. A few minutes after he left, we couldn't find Lucky. We eventually found him in his crate. He had gone to the place where he knew he was still boss. He was sitting inside pouting. You could see it on his face.

A part of the process was for us to spend about ten minutes a day with each dog, reinforcing the training. After every training session, Lucky would go pout in his pen. He really hated the next time the guy came a week later. He taught us to train the dogs the command for down. This meant they would sit and then lie down on voice command or hand signal. Down is a very submissive posture for a dog, or for any of us, for that matter. Even Charley did not like the training for down. Lucky hated it! Well, you know where he went as soon as we were finished with that session. You got it!

We went from sit/stay and down to come and teaching them to walk on heel. It is amazing to be able to walk and have your dog walk beside you without leading. Oh, they want to lead! You have to watch them or they will try to sneak out in front of you, especially Lucky.

Eventually, we had to put Lucky down because of lymphoma, but we still have Charley. You might have seen us. We often walk the mile from our house to Food Is Love for breakfast. Charley walks along with us and then sits or lies down beside us at the outside table. He likes the raisin toast. He doesn't jump on people coming in and out, even though they all stop to comment on how beautiful he is and how well behaved. "I wish my dog would do that," is the comment we get most of the time.

I was at the Vet's office a couple of days ago and Charley was just sitting beside me while everyone else's dogs were dragging them around the office. Charley looks at them with disdain. I wanted to say, "Folks, I'll teach you how to do this, if you want." I didn't…it would've sounded critical.

Dogs are so much more fun when they obey…kind of like kids.

CHAPTER 30--
GROCERIES, OUTHOUSES
AND CHEWING TOBACCO

My dad used to help out a man named John. It happened when I was pretty young and dad was preaching on Sunday afternoons at a little church called Grubbs' Mission in Hilda, South Carolina. A man started the mission in the community years before, because they didn't have a church. Other churches had since been started in the area, but the mission survived.

I have fond memories of that place, except that every Sunday I went to Sunday school and church at the Hagood Avenue Baptist Church in Barnwell and then after Sunday dinner, we would drive the seven miles to Hilda, then it was back to church for Sunday night service. It was a lot of church for a boy, but the mission was out in a rural area and had some neat stuff we didn't have at home.

It had an outhouse! Actually, it had two outhouses, a His'n and a Her'n. For those who don't know what that means, go read up on your Jeff Foxworthy material. Going to the bathroom was a real adventure. Since it was only used on Sundays, the wasps had plenty of time to build nests during the week. I don't know what it is about wasps, but they just love an outhouse. Just think about attempting to do your personal business while trying not to make any noises or sudden movements that might upset the wasps. You always kept one eye on the nest, no matter what else you were doing. Every now and then you would hear somebody yelling and they would come running from the outhouse, trying to get their pants up and stay ahead of the wasps at the same time. What fun!

We had running water at the mission, but it was also outside, and only ran when you pumped the handle. I would like to have a dollar for every time I pumped that handle. I pumped for everybody if they would let me. I loved that pump.

You are probably wondering why everybody was going to the bathroom and pumping water on the outside, when church was inside. Well, you seem to have forgotten about dinner on the ground. That's theological talk for a picnic. About once a month or so, we would have dinner on the ground. There was a shelter next to the church with tables and everything just like you find at the state park. Women would bring food, oh my, the food, and we would have dinner after church. Just thinking of the fried chicken and banana pudding makes me want to go back to the good old days. Unfortunately, you can't go back for just the good parts and the thought of those wasps and the fact that I can't run as fast as I used to, pulls me out of my little time warp and back to the present. What was I doing presently? Oh yeah, I was writing about my dad.

A man came into the mission every now and then, named John Curtis. He usually had pecans in his pocket and he would rattle them together as if he were pretending to have change. He was obviously poor and my dad found out that he had a wife and kids.

On several occasions I went with my dad to buy groceries for John and his family. We would go to the Piggly Wiggly and shop. Dad would buy a lot of necessities for the family, but then he would buy the kind of stuff that he bought for my sister and me, good stuff, cookies and candy. Then he would do what, for me, was the oddest and most wonderful thing, he would buy chewing tobacco for John. "Bull of the Woods," if I remember correctly. You see, my dad, from a religious perspective, was pretty much against drinking and smoking and chewing (he said the sickest he'd ever been was when he tried to learn to chew as a boy), but John chewed. My dad didn't use his own religious understanding to judge other people; he figured God already had that judge thing handled, so he didn't have to fool with it. It gave him more time to be kind, since he didn't have to be judge, too. And kindness is what it took to buy chewing tobacco for John, when dad wouldn't use it himself. He even had to risk letting somebody wonder why he was buying it.

Kindness is like that, it's not always easy, and it sometimes requires you to step out of your own comfort zone to do something for someone else. If it was easy to be kind, more people would be doing it.

It was amazing to drive up to that shack and begin hauling groceries in. The picture of the smiles on the faces of the kids when the good stuff came out of the bags is left to your imagination. I can't describe that.

You know, it's not natural to be kind and generous, that stuff is learned and passed down. My dad got it from Granny Agee. I hope you got it from somebody. If not, maybe you can start the legacy in your family. Now might be a good time for it.   Don't forget a plug of "Bull of the Woods."

CHAPTER 31--
MOTHER'S DAY

It's May already and one of the most important holidays of the year is in May. Can you guess what it is? Didn't you read it in the title? Of course, it's Mothers' Day! Where would we be without our mothers? Duh, not here, of course. Moms are the most important part of the creation process. I know, men, dads are important, too, but that's another holiday.

Moms not only protect us while we grow inside, but they begin to love us there. I believe it's a love that we experience, even though we can't remember it. Oh, but what about a mom who adopts a child? Their love starts out differently, but ends the same. It's a love that puts the child first, before everything else.

I once wrote a story about me going with my dad to buy and deliver groceries for a poor family. When I was writing that, all kinds of memories came back of my dad and me doing things together, especially fishing and hunting. I tried to think of mom memories and had trouble thinking of things we did together. I called my sister and we talked about it. Hers was a similar experience, we remembered mom always being there, but didn't remember big moments.

I thought about that for awhile, and finally figured things out. I can usually do that if I stop to think, unfortunately, I rarely do.

Dads got the big moments because they were at work most of the time. When you got to spend time with them, it was usually something special. Back then, moms were home all the time. They got you up for school, made breakfast, and were there when you got home. Sometimes it was cookies and milk or better yet, a chocolate cake and milk. They were there at suppertime hollering off the back porch that it was time to come eat. They took care of the scraped knees, the tears, and the little trouble you got into. It was a rare thing for mom to say, "Wait 'til your dad gets home!" Mom was doing the wash and hanging it on the clothes line; she was sprinkling and ironing. This was back before the days of double-knit and permanent press. She was giving the neighbor a permanent for her hair in the living room while they watched their stories. Boy those permanents sure did stink up the house. She was vacuuming and mopping and dusting, without any of the work-savers that we have today. Mom was reading Bible stories and talking about Jesus; she was there at night for prayers.

I especially remember my mom singing. She still has a beautiful alto voice and sang in the church choir when I was little. She would sing hymns at home as she did her work around the house. I would always listen for the words. She didn't always know the words, so she would make some up that fit into the song. Sometimes her words were better than the right ones. Sometimes she would hum in those places where her memory skipped.

Really, the big thing I remember about mom is the love. Being loved and cared for is what I remember most about my childhood; that was from mom and dad and my sister, but as I said, dads had to go to work, but mom was always there. Back then you only knew about the love from the hugs and stuff. It's only after you grow up that you see the love in all they did for you.

I realize, as I write this, that everyone did not have the same experience of love from their mom that I did. I am so sorry about that. I wish everyone could have the safety and security of knowing that you are always loved, no matter what. It's God's love, you know, a love that loves us good and loves us bad. It's a love that wants us good because it's best for us, but loves us either way.

For you moms reading this, Happy Mothers' Day! For the rest of you, if your mom is still living, call or go visit. She needs to know that you love her, too. For those whose mom is gone, she already knows.

CHAPTER 32--
NURSES WEEK

Last week was National Nurses Week. Guess what it was for? Yeah, it's set aside to honor nurses. Thought I would give you an easy one. I was going to write about them, but Mother's Day trumped Nurse's Week. Sorry about that, nurses. But many of you are moms, also, so you know the priority. Oh, I know, I know — some of you nurses are dads, too. I didn't mean to get into the politically incorrect area, there.

I love nurses (most of them). They do some of the most difficult work anyone could be asked to do, and they do it with a smile and a good attitude and compassion. OK, not all of them are like that; that's why I said I loved most of them. But what they do is not easy. The job itself is hard, but to do it with the above mentioned attributes is amazing.

Most nurses, especially the ones who work in the very intense areas such as the ER, the ICU and surgery, develop an oddly dark sense of humor to cope with the tragedies of life which they see every day. It was a sense of humor I loved, as I also worked among those tragedies.

The tragedies affect the rest of your life, too. For a long time I realized that I did not enjoy movies if they were dramas, and I never really understood why. Until one day, it hit me — my life is a drama. Drama doesn't entertain me; I need something funny to watch.

So sometimes we had to find funny in midst of tragedy. I remember once when a patient had died and no family was in town. They arrived the next day and wanted to see the deceased before he was released to the crematory. We tried to discourage this practice since our morgue was not a very pleasant place for visitation, but we accommodated the request when needed.

The nursing supervisor and I had pulled the gurney out of the cooler, unzipped the body bag and had covered the body with a sheet and a blanket up to his neck. We had gotten the call that the family was on their way when we were on break, so we went quickly to be sure things were ready. As we were waiting and talking, we suddenly realized that we were standing on either side of the gurney continuing to eat donuts and drink coffee over a dead body. We laughed and said something about how odd this would seem to most people.

One other time I was paged in the middle of the night for an impending death. Before I arrived the woman died and I guess the nursing supervisor had a very emotional husband on her hands. At one point she had escorted him back to the waiting room and then found him passed out in the stairwell and had to drag him through a doorway before she could get anyone to hear her calling for help. So this is what she has been through.

When I arrived at the ICU room, the man was standing beside his dead wife with his back to the door. The nursing supervisor was standing beside him and noticed me. She put her hand on his shoulder and said softly, "The chaplain is here." As she turned to leave, she walked past me, smiled and whispered, "Billy Bob." You don't really meet many people named Billy Bob these days, but I thought she was politely informing me of his name. She was so considerate that way.

Well, this man turns around and introduces himself, but his name was something else. So for a split second, I am feeling confused (which wasn't that unusual), and then he smiled.

Now, some of you are way ahead of me here. This man flashed the most amazing set of Billy Bob teeth I have ever seen; except they were not fake.

Now, as I am desperately trying to keep my composure in the middle of this man's tragedy, I hear snickering out in the nurses' station. It later turned to guffaws after the man left to go home. She really got me that time.

Anyway, I just wanted you to know that these angels of mercy have a dark side. So the next time you are in a hospital or doctor's office and hear laughter, it might be about you.

CHAPTER 33--
CRIMINAL
ORGANIZATIONS

For the last several years, a few federal government agencies have been trying to get some motorcycle clubs declared as criminal organizations by court decree. They've even wanted to call them homeland terrorists. They have infiltrated some of the clubs and arrested a few of the men on drug and/or weapons charges. The idea is that if they are declared criminal organizations, then if a crime is committed by any member of the club, then the rest of the club can be charged by association under the RICO laws.

Wow, this almost falls into the area of satire when you look at what has been happening in our country.

So, if this is the way it works, then the Masons and Rotary are criminal organizations, too, because of all of the lawyers and developers and CEO's of banks and insurance and mortgage companies who belong to those groups and have been involved in criminal activity. Some of them have even gone to prison for their actions. Therefore, if you follow the same standard, all of the members must be criminals. For surely they knew what was going on and supported it, right?

Then, there's the Roman Catholic Church. Hmmm? Here, you have priests who have been molesting children for years, if not decades, and you have bishops who have not only concealed it from the authorities, but have moved these men to places where they could commit the crime over and over again. So, I guess the entire church is a criminal organization, because, obviously, they knew what was happening.

Then, by association, you have all of the members of the church who have been supporting the criminal activity by giving their money to the church. Certainly, they must have known something about it. Doesn't that make sense? They all are criminals, I guess!

Well, what about BP? We're now finding out that the oil companies are crooked. Imagine that! And the federal agencies that were supposed to monitor them have somehow looked the other way. How did that happen, I wonder? Surely all of the executives and employees of BP should be charged with criminal activity. But what about all of the stockholders? They all have benefited from the criminal activity of BP. Shouldn't they share in the criminal responsibility?

Oh my, then you have Congress! Let's not even go there. But, instead, let's look at the federal law enforcement agencies themselves: the FBI, the CIA, ATF, DEA, the Border Patrol, Customs, etc, etc, etc. Of course, it makes sense that if one of their members commits any unlawful act, then the rest of them are involved, too. How could they not be, huh? That would surely include local law enforcement, wouldn't it?

Ok, have I been ridiculous enough, yet? Of course it's ridiculous to think that any member of an organization is responsible for the actions of some other member of the group.

It's so easy to target motorcycle clubs. They look like criminals, don't they? What with their long hair and beards and tattoos and dirty vests and don't forget their loud motorcycles. Everybody hates that! But, remember, none of that is against the law, and at least one of those hardcore 1% clubs invited me to join…if that tells you anything.

Also, remember that if the government can declare them a criminal organization, they can declare your group criminal when they decide they don't like you.

Of course there are probably more criminals in a hardcore motorcycle club than in Rotary. Motorcycle clubs draw a different type of person than the Rotary. But that doesn't make the club itself criminal. Club members aren't out raping and pillaging and assaulting innocent citizens.

Speaking of raping and pillaging; isn't it ironic that a credit card company uses that motif for their advertising campaign. They have that group that look like Huns running around destroying stuff as they try to fit into society. If there is any group that has been raping and pillaging the American people; it is certainly the credit card industry. How sad that our Congress, who could pass laws protecting us from these thieves, instead just take the donations to their campaign coffers and look the other way.

Some bike clubs may have some criminals, but they're not stealing millions from the American public like the drug dealers called pharmaceutical companies. They are not ripping you off every day like the insurance giants, so they can take millions in salary and benefits.

If you're going to look for criminal activity in our country, I think we would be better off starting to look from the top down rather than from the bottom up. Petty criminals do far less damage to our country than corporate criminals. Corporate criminals brought about our present recession and BP's greed has brought about an environmental catastrophe that will affect millions of working people.

Which is the criminal organization you are most afraid of?

CHAPTER 34-- THE EYE DOCTOR

I made appointments for Candy and me to see the eye doctor. That's not like the dentist where you go every six months or so (or is it six years?) to get your teeth cleaned. I'll deal with dentists in another story, but eye appointments are usually a reminder that you're getting older and can't see what you once could. We usually put these off until we can't see our watch to tell the time or see the TV, you know, the important stuff. Maybe we went to get our Driver's License renewed and couldn't read line 5 in that little machine they make you look in.

Once, my dad, who couldn't see a thing without his glasses, went to get his renewed. He had to stand in line behind several people who had to read line 5. He kept hearing them read the same letters. When it was his turn, the lady said, "Why don't you try first without your glasses." So he took his glasses off and felt around for the machine and looked in. He said he couldn't even see line 1, which is that really, really big letter E. The lady said, "Read line 5," and Dad repeated from memory the letters he had heard everyone else say. She was so pleased and gushed, "See, now you don't have the eyeglass restriction on your license." Dad laughed when he told me about it and said something about not being able to find the car without his glasses, much less drive.

Anyway, this time I went to see "King and King" who go to our church. They, the office staff, and the opticians were wonderful.

Back when I was thirty-eight or so, I had to get my first pair of glasses. When I couldn't recognize what I was eating, I figured it was time. Basically I was going to get bifocals because my arm had gotten too short. Most of you know what I mean. There is a point where you can hold something far enough away to almost be able to read it, but now it is too far and you still can't see it. Time for bifocals…glasses for the chronologically gifted.

Back then the doctor wanted me to try those transition or vanity lenses that don't have lines in them. I wasn't that vain, but he thought they were the right choice for me. "Try them for a month," he said, "some people like them." How'd that go? Yeah, not even close. If you've ever had them, you might know what I mean. They don't work for some of us.

When I tried to find the right spot to see through, I looked like someone with Parkinson's disease or one of those bobble-head dogs that you use to see in the back of a car window. My head would bob up and down searching for clarity. If I turned my head sideways, everything would move in waves and I got sea-sick; nearly threw up a few times.

Preaching for a month with those glasses on was nothing but fun. The congregation loved it. I would look down to read the scripture… bob, bob, bob. Then I would look back up…up, down, up, down. Things never were clear and I'm not just talking about my theology. People in the center of the lens were in focus, but everyone in the peripheral was blurry. Now, it might have been that those folks sitting out on the edge were just blurry on their own, I don't know, maybe that's why they sit out there. Anyway, I couldn't get used to it. So, I took the glasses back and got good old bifocals and loved them.

Unfortunately, it wasn't long before two lenses were not enough. I could read close up and I could see at a distance, but I couldn't see in that middle range. You don't realize how many things in life are in that middle range; things like computer screens, speedometers, grocery shelves, people's faces, and everything else that I really needed to see. It seemed like nothing important was in the close or distance range. Everything was in the middle.

So, they added a third lens to my already full glasses. I wish they would just give me one big middle range lens. It seems to be the only one I need.

You know what? I wish there were some spiritual glasses we could wear. Sometimes I think things get a little blurry when we are making decisions about right and wrong or what to say. You know what I think would help...if we played that little game the eye doctor plays. You know the one; "Is this one better or this one? Which is better, number 1 or number 2?" If we stopped to consider our decisions before we made them, I think we might make better ones. And, wow, what if we did that before we spoke? "Which is better, say something positive or negative? Should I compliment or complain? Should I speak or keep my mouth shut?" How great would that be? A lot more of us would probably say things that are more positive and complimentary and some of us would decide to keep our mouths shut. That would be a good thing!

CHAPTER 35--
MY DAD'S DEATH
AND RELATIONSHIPS

This was written in August, 2008.

My dad died on May 20, 2008 at 9:30 in the morning as I lay by his side and Mom stood by the bed. He had gotten up to have coffee with us and then wanted to lie down. He turned 82 on March 24th and celebrated his 62nd anniversary with my mom on May 14th. They didn't get to go out as they planned because he was weak. He was diagnosed with stomach cancer on July 12, 2004.

We expected he would not live very long, so within the first year, he visited with his brothers and sisters more than he had in the last few decades. That's one of the nice things about a terminal disease, you get to do things you might not have done if you didn't know death was coming. What my dad chose to do was see people he loved.

I recently watched "The Bucket List," which is a movie about two men with terminal diagnoses who decide to make a list of things they want to do before they kick the bucket. In the process of doing things like driving race cars and skydiving, and going places they'd never been, they also experience life. What all of the things and places do, is to move them back to understanding the importance of relationships; one with his wife, the other with an estranged daughter and grand-daughter he had never met. If you haven't seen it, I recommend it.

In November 2007, my first District Superintendent (sort of like a bishop) died. His son was a college friend and we moved to seminary together with our wives and lived in some duplexes as neighbors. He wrote me and said that when his dad was dying, he told him to remember that the important thing in life is relationships.

Are you starting to see a pattern here?

Relationships! That's what we value as our life is drawing to a close. It's not about where we've been, or what we've done, or how much money we have or don't have. It's about relationships. That's what we value.

I wonder why we don't value them more while we are living rather than just when we are dying.

You know, they always tell us to live everyday as if it were our last. But if I thought tomorrow was my last, I probably wouldn't go to work. I would probably spend it with people I love, and I would do that the next day and the next and the next, because it might be my last. After a while, not only would we be looking for a place to live and something to eat, since I would have lost my job, but those I love would be getting tired of hanging around just in case it was my last day.

We would actually think someone was nuts if they lived everyday as if it were their last.

So, how do we value relationships without driving our friends and family crazy; without becoming morbid and morose? I'm not sure, but let me tell you about some things.

The day before my dad died, a former pastor and wife, who were at our church when I was a teenager (if that gives you some idea of a time frame), drove three hours to see him. They spent about an hour with us. I called Rev. Jesse Sims the next morning to tell him Dad died. He said he had been saying for several weeks that he needed to get down to see dad. He sure was glad he came when he did. So was Dad and so were we. It was a special afternoon!

Someone else called my mom, after they heard the news, and said they had been planning to come that afternoon. Mom said, "You waited too late." I thought it was kind of a cruel thing to say until I heard they had been planning to come for two years. Maybe they needed to hear that you can plan too long.

Recently, a friend's mom died up north. I called a couple of times to check on him. I was talking with a mutual friend who said, "I thought about calling, but I don't want to be a bother." I said, "Call anyway; everybody says they meant to." He called. When the friend returned, he was thanking me for calling and mentioned the other man. "It meant so much that he took the time to call. A lot of people said they were thinking about me, but that's easy to say. How do I know they were if they didn't call?" Exactly!!

It seems to mean so much to people when I call them on their birthday. I take time everyday to pull up the birthdays that are in our church computer and call. Some of them haven't been to church in over two years or more. I call anyway. Sometimes, when I say, "This is Pastor Herb." They say, "Who?" That's a dead giveaway. Once they realize I'm not calling to ask for money or to fuss at them for not coming to church, they're relieved. I tell them, "I'm calling to say Happy Birthday!" They are surprised and thrilled. Why? Why would it be important to someone to be called by a pastor they don't know from Moses? Because it makes them feel valuable; valued in a relationship with the church they've neglected and maybe forgotten. They've been remembered. It's why I call; they are valuable; they are important. (By the way, if you want a call, send your name, birthday and phone number to padre@ stfrancishelps.com)

When people heard my dad died, some called me. Others sent flowers, or cards, or emails, or chose other ways to remember me and honor my dad. I read every card, email and every name. Some people sent two cards. I think they forgot they sent the first one. That was okay. It meant they were thinking of me enough to take the time to find a card, sign it, address it and mail it, maybe twice. That's a lot of thinking about me. I loved it.

What does all this mean? How do we live when tomorrow might or might not be our last day? How do we value relationships without people thinking we're crazy? I'll tell you. Call somebody who comes to mind. Remember people on purpose! Grandparents, parents, children, grandchildren, brothers, sisters, aunts and uncles, cousins and friends all want to know they are important to you.

HERB AGEE

My biker friend, Boodan, goes down his phone list every so often and calls everybody just to say, "Hi, I'm thinking about you and I love you." Wow! I know he means it when he takes the time to call.

You don't have to say a lot. You might try it with your family and friends. Remember, one of these days will be your last!!! Don't miss your chance.

CHAPTER 36--
MY WIFE, THE
HOSPICE DOCTOR

My wife is Dr. Carmel Lee Quigley. Her friends and co-workers call her Candy, but I still call her Dr. Quigley. Formerly she was an Emergency Room Physician. That's where we first met. I was the chaplain at Wuesthoff Hospital in Rockledge, Florida and she worked the ER. It was amazing to watch her. She's 4'11" but walks every bit of 6'4" in an ER where she is in charge. She commanded great respect from the people who worked with her. I said, commanded, not demanded. She deserved every bit of respect she received.

For the first five years we worked together, working was our only relationship. I was the chaplain she called when a crisis came into the ER. I was in the ER a lot anyway, because I loved the excitement. I had been an orderly in an ER in Nashville between college and seminary, an EMT on an ambulance for a few years, and later a chaplain in training in the ER at Tampa General Hospital. So, I loved the ER.

But...the ER was a different place when Dr. Quigley was there.

Some of the nurses called her a magneto de caca, which was a bad Spanish translation suppose to mean something about the most terrible stuff coming in when she was working. We were a small town hospital, but when Dr. Quigley worked, it was heart attacks, stabbings, shootings, overdoses and car wrecks. They could have easily done a blockbuster TV show just about her shifts.

On top of the terrible stuff, there was a constant flow of Medicaid moms who refused to go to the health department and only brought their children in when Dr. Quigley was working, because they knew their kids would get the loving care and concern they deserved, whether they could pay or not.

She was also a great teacher and nurses loved to listen to her talk to the patient and families because they learned so much as she taught about their condition. Many doctors talk medical jargon and nurses used to say, "She's the only doc we don't have to translate for...to tell the patient and family what she meant."

I listened to her teach a patient one day, who had come in with chest pain. I was sitting at a computer and overheard the conversation. The patient appeared to be in his early 60's, but had the rough look of a life lived hard.

As Dr. Quigley approached his bedside, he whined, "I know, I know, Doc. I need to quit drinking and smoking and need to lose weight." He seemed to expect to be criticized. Candy countered, "Not necessarily." He looked confused, "What do you mean?" She continued, "You're an adult. You get to choose how you want to live your life. Some people choose to live for gusto and some choose to live for mileage." He perked up, "Yeah, I have lived for gusto." She said, "And that's okay, but you need to remember that if you choose to live for gusto, you probably won't get as many miles."

While they were waiting for the results of his tests; she was walking by his room. He called, "Hey, doc, I have a question." She walked over to his bedside and he asked, "What do I need to do if I want a few more miles?" She smiled, "Well, that's a good question. You may have gusto-ed past the point of no return, but you may choose to give up some gusto and hope it turns into a few more miles."

I loved how she showed him the respect he deserved that he didn't expect. She also empowered him to be responsible for his own health by his own choices. I don't think he had ever looked at it the way she presented it.

My guess is that some of you are thinking about your own choices, right now; considering the gusto vs. mileage idea. I vote for gusto! Here we go!

Anyway, I'm running out of room and am going to need a second part of this story. I haven't even gotten to the hospice part yet.

CHAPTER 37--
MY WIFE THE HOSPICE
DOCTOR-PART 2

The last part ended with Candy teaching a man about the difference in living for gusto or mileage and the possible consequences of each.

Her teaching one day included a variety of people. We had not had a trauma in awhile since a trauma center had opened close to us. Many of our newer staff had not dealt with serious trauma. On this day a young man had been stabbed in the heart by his brother and because he was being resuscitated at the time, they could not fly him to the larger hospital.

As the crew awaited his arrival by ambulance, she said, "This mother can lose two sons, one to death and one to prison, we have to do everything we can to save this kid."

Candy commented that they would probably have to crack his chest. A younger ER physician working that day said, "I never did that in my training." As the young man was placed on the gurney, she handed the scalpel to the younger doctor and said, "You're going to do this one." She walked him through the procedure of cutting and spreading the ribs so she could get her hands inside his chest. (We have an x-ray of her hands around his heart.) A heart surgeon came down to help and took the man to surgery. He died the next day, but many on staff learned to do something they had never done before, which might have saved the next one who needed their expertise.

HERB AGEE

She left that hospital and then three more before she found hospice. Unfortunately, hospitals want ER doctors to use a cattle prod instead of a stethoscope. They just want them to move the meat. If a patient needs to be admitted to the hospital, then get them admitted. If they don't need to be admitted, then get them out. It's all about wait time. This isn't said to disparage hospitals; they're working within a very narrow margin of profit and times have changed since Candy started in ER medicine. It just means that their way of taking care of patients didn't fit with her way anymore.

Candy had often said that when it was time to wind down from emergency medicine, she might like to work for a hospice. Well, at Christmas of 2006, Candy's mom was with us in Englewood. She had an annoying little cough that wouldn't go away. When she went home to Fort Myers, they did x-rays and a cat scan and nothing was showing. As the cough continued, they did a bronchial scope on February 14th and found lung cancer. They started treatment immediately, but she deteriorated very rapidly and went into the ICU in March and then a hospice house April 4. It was with Hope Hospice in Cape Coral on Wednesday evening and Candy called me Thursday morning to say, "Herb, I want to do this now; I love this place."

Lee Quigley died the next morning, April 6, 2007 on Good Friday. As Candy and her sister, Lorie, left the hospice house, Lorie said, "It's just like mom, always the over achiever, she had to die on the same day as Jesus." You'd have to know Lorie. As they laughed together in the parking lot, it started to rain. Lorie laughed and said, "As if we don't look bad enough."

Candy came home and went online and found that Tidewell Hospice and Palliative Care was looking for a physician. She was hired, but there's another story I'll have to write later about that process.

Of hospice, she says, "I get to spend an hour with my patients and families now instead of ten minutes." Tidewell says, "We can't add days to your life, but we can add life to your days." I wondered what it would be like for her to be caring for people who were in the process of dying rather than trying to save them. She said the most amazing thing, "What a privilege and sacred journey to carry them to the finish line and hand them over."

Dr. Quigley is smart and funny. One ER physician, who was sixty-five years old, told me, "She's the smartest ER doc I've ever worked with and I've been doing this quite awhile." He's also the one who was writing down her funny Quigley-isms so he could remember them. If you remember any of your favorites, send them to me.

Speaking of Quigley-isms, one day I was visiting a member of our church and the Certified Nursing Assistant from hospice was there. When she found out that Candy was my wife, she said, "Dr. Quigley doesn't even work out of our office, but we have some of her sayings posted on the wall. One of those sayings changed my life." I was impressed and should have left it at that, but instead, I asked, "Which saying?" To which she responded, "You can't polish a turd." Everyone in the room laughed, and I'm thinking, "How bad does your life have to be that this bit of wisdom is life changing." So I asked, "How did that change your life?" She smiled, "I was trying to polish one at the time, but when I read that, I kicked him out."

Although I had never heard that phrase before Candy used it, evidently it has been around. A few weeks after my encounter with the CNA, Candy came home laughing. She said that during their weekly Interdisciplinary Team meeting, the chaplain, who always gave a devotion of some type, brought a video clip from the Discovery Channel show, Myth Busters. The clip was about the myth, "You can't polish a turd." Well, you guessed it; they found that a certain animal type, mixed with dirt, could actually be polished.

Well, I can tell you, she didn't wind down, but she sure loves hospice.

CHAPTER 38--
CANDY'S HOSPICE JOB

I've never written about how Candy started working for Tidewell. This goes back to 2007. We already knew that Candy's job at the Englewood Hospital was in jeopardy. The group that Candy worked for was losing the ER contract. She had not heard from the new group about whether they wanted her to stay. She did not know if she would have a place to work or not.

Charlotte Regional Hospital, where she had filled in some, was a possibility, but for only two or three shifts a month. In the middle of all of this chaos, Candy's mom was diagnosed with lung cancer on February 14th.

Well, for the last several years, Candy had commented that she might like to work in hospice when she was ready to wind down from the excitement of ER. The day after her mom went into the hospice house in Cape Coral; Candy called me and said, "I want to do this now." When she came home Friday morning, April 6, after her mom died, she went online and found a Hospice Fellowship position available at Moffitt in Tampa. She interviewed the next Tuesday, but found out on Thursday that they were choosing another younger candidate. She was really disappointed and felt very old and unwanted.

I went online and discovered that Tidewell Hospice was looking for a physician. She called and left a message and emailed an application on Thursday night and was disappointed that no one responded on Friday. I told her the director might be off on Friday.

What a terrible weekend for her.

Well, on Tuesday, Tidewell called and apologized because they thought someone was getting in touch with her on Friday. They wanted her to come in immediately for an interview. She interviewed that afternoon and they wanted her.

In the meantime...the director of the ER in Punta Gorda called with the news that one of their doctors was leaving and they had a full-time position open and they wanted Candy really badly and were offering a raise over Englewood.

Then, the new group taking over Englewood Hospital got in touch with her and said they thought she was staying with them and bumped the salary up to match Punta Gorda.

Then...Moffitt called back and told her that when their board looked at the candidates, they overruled the committee decision and offered the position to Candy.

From no job to four really great opportunities in just a few days. Amazing!!

CHAPTER 39-- GOING TO THE DENTIST

I went to the dentist recently. I have a great dentist now, but I've had my share of real losers through the years. As a child, I remember a dentist who looked like a bear. His arms were so hairy that it was scary for a young boy.

The other problem was that he tried to hide things from you. When he was coming to give me a shot, he had the syringe down beside his leg and would only bring it up after he had my head back and mouth open. It didn't help; I knew what was coming.

My best dentist was when I was in high school. He was a good friend, too. Some of you reading this will remember him. He was killed in a car wreck…God bless Dr. Dyches.

Dentists for kids are completely different now. When Scott was little, we found a pediatric dentist. Other parents said he was great. They had video games in the waiting room; that was cool. They really didn't want parents to come back with the kids, but I insisted. I'm glad I did. They gave Scott a little elixir to drink and put him in a chair in a row of about eight chairs. He quickly fell asleep and the dentist moved from chair to chair as the assistants worked in between. Scott might have been there for 10-15 minutes. He slept the rest of the day. We never went back.

I see why most parents loved it. They found a place to drop their kid and after a few minutes of dentistry they could take them home where the kid would sleep off the medicine, giving them some free time.

Scott wasn't that kind of kid…I mean the kind you preferred to be asleep. Scott was fun to have around. He was an only child, which meant he was around a lot of adults and had an adult vocabulary, and he had a very high IQ. He was always fun to talk with. And, he wouldn't have liked the drug the kid method of dentistry, anyway. He liked to know what was going on so he could deal with it honestly.

We found a regular dentist who was good with kids like Scott. He would explain what he was going to do, show them the tools, be honest about any pain or discomfort to expect and would then be as gentle as possible. Scott really liked his style. Scott always appreciated fairness and honesty. I guess we all do. I'm not sure why we don't offer it to our kids more often.

When he was four, he came to me one day and said, "Dad, I need to talk with you." You never knew what that meant. I asked what he wanted. He continued, "I don't think I believe in Santa Claus anymore." I asked if any of his friends had been talking about that and he said they hadn't. I questioned, "Why don't you think you believe in him anymore?" He seemed sure, "I don't see how one man can get all around the world in one night." I assured him that it was okay if he didn't believe in Santa Claus, but I asked, "Where do the presents come from?" He just looked at me, "I haven't figured that part out, yet." I told him that a lot of other kids still believed and for him not to tell them his doubts and he thought that was good. He seemed to not want to burst their bubble.

I've often wondered why we lie to kids so much about stuff like that; Santa Claus, the Easter Bunny, the Tooth Fairy. One of my favorite Calvin and Hobbes cartoons deals with the topic.

Calvin: This whole Santa Claus thing just doesn't make sense. Why all the secrecy? Why all the mystery? If the guy exists, why doesn't he ever show himself and prove it? And if he doesn't exist, what's the meaning of all this?

Hobbs: I dunno…isn't this a religious holiday?

Calvin: Yea, but actually, I've got the same questions about God.

When kids find out we're lying about many of their childhood fantasies, why would they believe anything we say? Even about God.

Wow! I really went far afield from the dentist. But, just one more thought about Scott. When he was pretty little, I told him, "Scott, you always have the right to question my decision, if you don't argue. You can always say, 'Dad, can I tell you what I think?'" Over the years, I found that to be an amazingly wise parental decision. I'm not sure if I thought of it or if I read it somewhere. But, often, when I told Scott something, he would ask, "Dad, can I tell you what I think?" After I listened to what he was thinking, I would sometimes say, "Wow, that's better than what I thought." It just took listening with an open mind, rather than being in the middle of an argument.

I listened and often took his suggestion, and on those times when I thought my way was better I would say, "Scott, I know you see it differently, but this time we need to do it my way." He never argued. He knew he had been heard and his opinion considered. His mom once said to me when he was young, "I hate arguing with Scott; he always makes so much sense." I thought, "Hmmmm." I suggested she listen before the argument starts. Once the argument starts, as a parent, you feel like you have to win.

For those young parents reading this story; the information you are receiving is worth its weight in gold. Everyone feels better when you listen and respect their opinion; even kids.

Oh, well, I guess we'll look at dentists some other time.

CHAPTER 40--
HOW I STARTED RIDING

You know, when people find out I ride a motorcycle, they often ask me when I started riding. When I tell them 2004, they usually ask what possessed me to start. It's a good question, especially from people who knew me before. It's pretty unlike me. Here's the story.

As a hospital chaplain in Rockledge, Florida, I often was involved with bikers who came in from wrecks or other injuries they tend to get. In 1996, one of the Warlocks came in with a head injury from an accident during the annual toy run held in Brevard County. Dr. Quigley was the ER physician that Sunday afternoon and I was paged in to assist. (Dr. Quigley and I were not involved at the time.)

Boodan, who seemed to be the representative of the Warlocks at the moment, came to me and said, "A lot of brothers will be showing up, but if anybody starts to get out of hand, please let me handle it instead of calling the police." I was glad to oblige and he also asked if he could see his brother. I told him I would need to check with the doctor. Candy came out and stood toe to toe with him. He's 6'2" and she's 4'11" so it was quite a picture. He asked politely if he could see his brother. Candy thought he was family and said, "Of course." When Boodan came in, he found his friend unconscious on a ventilator. Candy told him that his friend might be able to hear, so it was okay to talk to him. Boodan leaned down close to his ear and said, "You drive like sh--." It doesn't sound so comforting to most of us, but something sentimental would have made the patient think he was dying. We weren't sure about it at the time, but Boodan's greeting would have made him feel that he was okay.

I later took Boodan and another Warlock up to the waiting room. He said that someone needed to be close. This was back when the clubs were fighting a lot.

When we walked into the waiting room, there was a large African American family there. It was Sunday, so they were all dressed in their finest church attire. Boodan and his brother were not. They looked like they would just as soon rip off your head and spit down your neck as not.

We stepped into a small private room and talked awhile. Because they had not eaten, I found the number for pizza delivery and they ordered something. I stepped out to answer another page and later ran into the delivery person looking for them. I walked him to the waiting room and they invited me to eat. I didn't have time and excused myself to another call.

When I returned, Boodan and his friend had stepped out, but the other family was eating pizza. I jokingly asked, "What's going on, here?" One of them answered, "They ordered us a pizza. When they walked in, they looked pretty scary, but they are really nice guys." I laughed.

The next day, I was in the room of the girlfriend who was also involved in the accident. She was only suffering from severe road rash, extremely painful, but she was not in the ICU. As we talked, a group of the brothers walked in. One of them told her not to worry about their rent or other bills…things would be taken care of by the club until they were okay.

As I listened, I thought to myself, "That's how the church ought to be. We should be able to take care of one another when needed." Then I realized the difference. The church would have trouble knowing how to end the help. It would be easy for someone to continue to milk the injury and take advantage of the kindness. The brothers would never let that happen. They didn't have to worry about hurting anybody's feelings. If he was taking advantage of the club he would get his butt kicked.

Sometimes I think we need a butt-kicking committee in the church. Wow, would they be busy!!

Anyway, the brother recovered from his head injury and my contact with the Warlocks ended for awhile. It wasn't until April of 2003 that we were brought together again by the tragedy of a death.

That part of the story will have to wait until next time.

CHAPTER 41--
HOW I STARTED
RIDING--PART 2

I left out part of the story from being in the waiting room with Boodan and his brother. I mentioned that we talked awhile, but I didn't go into any detail. Boodan said it was okay to tell it.

While we were talking, Boodan said, "I was studying to be a preacher once." I asked him what happened. This was his response, "I was in a drug rehab center in Texas that was run by a church. During that time I was saved and felt a call to preach and started taking Bible classes. I studied for awhile, but after I got involved with the inner workings of the church, I found out they were interested in the same thing the club was interested in...money and power. I decided to hang with the guys who were at least honest about it."

I told him I knew some churches were like that, but I was really sorry it had been his experience. Who can defend that? I didn't even try.

He later told me that while he was preparing for ministry, God had given him a dream to start a Christian Motorcycle Club. It was to be called the Lord's Heave. This came from a King James translation of the Old Testament about a special offering to God. The offering was called the Lord's Heave, or Heave Offering. It was lifted up...thus the heave. The dream is yet to be fulfilled. Boodan has often asked me to start the club, but my answer is always, "It's not my dream, but yours. Maybe someday, God will let you fulfill your dream."

Anyway, I ended the last part of the story mentioning a tragic death in April of 2003 that brought us together again. It was Sunday afternoon and Candy and I were driving to Melbourne for a Vince Gill concert. I received a page about a death from a motorcycle accident that had come into the ER. He came in as a John Doe, but we found out it was the son of one of our nurses, and she was unaware of his death. We went to the hospital and spent the rest of the day with his family. We were told that he was riding a motorcycle because he had become a member of the Warlocks Motorcycle Club.

The next day I went to their house and Boodan was there. Boodan had gotten Keith into the club and considered him a best friend. He was there to offer the condolences and assistance of the club. He was obviously grieving the death of a brother. We talked with the family and found that Keith would be cremated. I was asked to do the eulogy at the funeral, which would be held at a Catholic church.

After that meeting, Boodan told me they wanted a Warlock patch to be on Keith when he was cremated. I knew the owners of the funeral home and crematory, so I told Boodan I would see that it was done. The next day, I met him at his apartment to pick up the patch. As he handed it to me, he said, "Please don't let anyone else handle this." For those of you who have not hung around 1% motorcycle clubs; there is a sacredness with which they view their patch. I told him that I understood. I said, "I have vestments that are considered sacred, even though they're made out of plain material. What they represent is what makes them special."

The owner had given me the time and place of the cremation and I was able to go and personally place the patch on Keith right as he was going in. The effort I made to help and the respect I gave the patch formed an immediate bond with Boodan. At the funeral, I also gave the brothers the opportunity to speak during the eulogy.

A couple of weeks later, the club was having an auction at the clubhouse to raise money for Keith's family. Boodan invited me to come for that and a month later, invited me back for the patch burning. This was where Keith would be honored and his personal vest and colors burned.

When the final rituals were over, I assumed our relationship would become dormant until our paths crossed again by some other tragedy.

I was wrong. Boodan began calling me every now and then to meet for lunch. Our friendship continued to grow.

It grew to the place where I felt comfortable enough to ask him to use his truck to transport a ping pong table from Cocoa to Orlando for me. This was late November and I bought one for Christmas, thinking it would fit in my van. Wrong, again. Anyway, we drove to Orlando and I called Candy to let her know Boodan would be with me. The original hospital incident happened in 1996 and Candy and I were married in 2000. This was 2003.

Candy fixed supper for us and as we were sitting at the table, Boodan innocently commented, "Padre, you need to come hang out at the strip club with me sometime." Candy quickly replied, "It's bad for his heart." Boodan questioned, "How is it bad for his heart?" Candy quipped, "He might get a steak knife in it!!" Boodan literally fell on the floor laughing.

Our lunches continued through December and we even had dinner together on New Year's Eve as Candy was busy working the evening shift in the ER.

It would be January 2nd that our friendship would be cemented through another accident. Eventually I'll get to how I started riding, which was the premise of this story when it began. Who knew it would get this long?

CHAPTER 42--
HOW I STARTED
RIDING--PART 3

ended part 2 mentioning that Boodan and I had dinner together on New Year's Eve. In the early evening of Friday, January 2, 2004, my pager went off in Orlando. It was Sharon, the secretary in our emergency room. She said, "Herb, I just received a strange call from a highway patrolman. He said that somebody named Budda or something had been in a bad motorcycle accident and while he was still lying on the ground he asked the patrolman to call the Padre and Dr. Quigley."

Well, he really didn't know who the Padre was, but he knew Dr. Quigley, so he called the ER.

I asked Sharon, "Boodan?" "Yea, that's it," she said. I asked where he was and she told me he had been taken to Cape Canaveral Hospital in Cocoa Beach. Well, Candy heard me and asked what was going on. When I told her, she said, "Let's go!" I knew I was going, but didn't know she was. We jumped in the van for the forty-five minute drive to the hospital.

Cape Canaveral Hospital was not a trauma center, and I knew that if Boodan was alive and seriously injured, he would have been flown to one. So, one of two scenarios was being played out. Either he was not too serious and could be transported to a local hospital, or he was dying and they were trying to resuscitate him and therefore he could not be flown but had to be transported to the nearest hospital by ambulance.

As we were driving, rather rapidly, down the Beeline (now called the Beachline), I called the hospital's Vice President of Nursing, Jan McCoy, who just happened to be a member of our church. I asked her to find out how Boodan was and to grease the wheels for us, since this was not our hospital. She called back to say he was okay and they were expecting us.

When we arrived, the place was crawling with Warlocks. They were loading Boodan's bike in the back of someone's truck. Someone had turned right in front of him at the hospital entrance. I spoke to a couple of the brothers and Candy and I went in.

Candy knew most of the nurses because they had worked with her at Wuesthoff, and we were escorted back to Boodan's room and met Tanya, his girlfriend. Boodan had a broken leg and badly broken wrist and was in a lot of pain. Tanya said they had not given him anything for the pain yet. Hmm, how can I put this delicately? Let me just say that Candy made sure someone immediately gave him pain medication.

The X-ray tech brought the wrist film out for Candy to see. The ER doc then said there was no one locally who could fix his wrist, but there was a doctor in Orlando who was willing to see him. Candy asked, "Who?" When she was told Dr. White, Candy said, "That's who we want." The doctor commented that unfortunately, being a Friday night, there was a four hour wait for a transport ambulance. Candy said, "Oh, no way, we'll take him in our van."

So, we loaded a drugged Boodan, with a wrapped broken leg and a wrapped broken wrist, into our Chrysler mini-van and headed out for Orlando with Tanya. When we arrived at the Orlando Regional Medical Center ER on a Friday night somewhere close to midnight, it looked like a zoo. It reminded me of one of those buses in a third world country with people hanging out of the doors and riding on the roof and bumpers. By the way, Boodan remembers nothing of this night after Candy got him medicated.

I went in and got a wheelchair. We loaded Boodan in and Candy took off through the outer door. When she got to the locked door that goes from the lobby to the actual ER, she yelled, "Open the *******, door." Whoever was sitting near the button, did just that! As we walked into the treatment area, a doctor looked up and said, "Candy Quigley, you haven't grown an inch!" It turns out she used to work at the ORMC

ER and taught residents. The doctor asked why she was there and when she told him, they took someone out of an exam room, put them in the hallway, and put Boodan into that room.

Dr. White arrived and remembered Candy, too (she's pretty unforgettable). He straightened the wrist by using some twilight sleep medication and wrapped it again. He said he would have to wait until Monday to do surgery because of the swelling. Another orthopedic surgeon would see him then to schedule surgery for his leg. They sent him home with orders to return to a different Orlando hospital on Monday morning for Dr. White to perform the surgery.

This meant we had to get him back home. He was awakening from the twilight sleep and was beginning to experience some pain. We stopped at our house in Orlando to make him a couple of peanut butter sandwiches. He wolfed them down along with some coffee, which allowed us to get some pain meds into a stomach that wouldn't refuse them now, if you know what I mean. Please don't puke in the van.

We got him home to Cocoa Beach at 6:00 on Saturday morning and his sons met us at the apartment to help get him in. Once he was in bed, we returned home. We went over on Saturday afternoon so Candy could administer some medication to prevent blood clots. She had a nurse stop by on Sunday.

Candy had to work on Monday, but I drove Boodan back to Orlando for his surgery to learn that, oh my, they didn't have him on the schedule. Wait until you hear how that played out.

If you can hang in there, we'll eventually get to how I started riding.

CHAPTER 43--
HOW I STARTED
RIDING--PART 4

O kay, Monday morning, Tanya, Boodan and I arrived at Sand Lake Hospital in Orlando. Sand Lake was a part of the ORMC system. I got Boodan inside and then parked the van. When I got back in, there was already a disturbance. Note to self...don't leave Boodan alone for very long. The woman in charge of checking people in was not the most pleasant person you've ever met. She surely was not impressed with Boodan.

I asked what the problem was and she informed me that he was not on the surgery schedule. I thought this might happen. Dr. White saw Boodan sometime on Saturday morning and his office would not have been open on the weekend. They would not have been able to talk with the scheduling people, yet. It really didn't call for the rudeness we were experiencing.

I stepped outside and called Candy and told her what was going on. She said, "Let me make a call and I'll call you back." She called me back in a few minutes to say that Dr. White was having his office call the hospital right now." I went back in and told the lady the office would be calling. She came out from the back in a few minutes and said the office called and Boodan would be worked in at the end of Dr. White's schedule. She expected that to be somewhere between three and five o'clock. I asked her where Boodan could wait and she said he would have to sit in the waiting room because there was no where else to put him.

I stepped outside and called Candy and told her what was going on. She said, "Let me make a call and I'll call you back." Sound familiar? She called me back in a few minutes to say that she had called the woman who use to be the nursing supervisor at Sand Lake, but she was no longer working there. She was, however, the VP of Nursing over all of the ORMC system. She was not in her office, but Candy explained our problem to her secretary. The secretary said she would call Sand Lake.

Well, I went back in and told Boodan and Tanya what was happening and we waited for a few minutes, not knowing what to expect. Boodan was ready to head home. Suddenly, our previously rude receptionist came out with a completely new attitude. She couldn't do enough for us. She had made arrangements for Boodan to go to a special, private waiting area that had big lounge chairs so he and we could be comfortable. She would let Dr. White's staff know where he was so they could find him when it was time for the surgery. It's amazing what an attitude adjustment can do.

After surgery, Boodan stayed at Sand Lake for a few days. You can be sure the rest of the staff had heard about him. They didn't know why he was a VIP, but they just knew he was. He even had visits from the chaplains there. He ended up having surgery on his leg the next day.

Because of Candy, he went from being treated like trash to being treated like royalty. It's how we all should be treated, by the way. You can imagine what Boodan thinks of Candy. She had only officially met him the one time at our house and yet was pulling all of her strings to see that he was treated properly. He thinks she walks on water. She does, sometimes.

I transported him home when it was time to get out and Tanya and his sons took over his care. I assumed that our relationship would go back to lunches every now and then. Wrong! Boodan, through this experience, considered us a part of his family. He said that nobody, even his club brothers, had ever taken care of him like we had. I reminded him that some of his brothers had come over to Orlando and sat with Tanya and me the first night when Candy and Dr. White were in the back straightening his wrist. I reminded him of all of the things they had been doing since that night.

I finally said, "Boodan, all of your brothers and friends have done everything they were able to do, but none of them are doctors who have a reputation in the Central Florida area to get things done like Candy. They did what they could do; we did what we could do. It's just that this time, what she could do was what was needed."

Anyway, that experience cemented our friendship so that Boodan and Tanya became a regular part of our life. But, I think it was six months later in June, with Boodan sitting on the couch at our house watching TV, that the first conversation about me riding took place.

Part 5 is next.

CHAPTER 44--
HOW I STARTED
RIDING--PART 5

While we were watching TV one night, Boodan said, "Padre, you need to get a bike so you can ride to Sturgis with me this August." For those of you unaware, Sturgis, South Dakota has the largest bike rally in the country. I looked at Boodan and said (with great respect), "Are you crazy?" Candy chimed in, "No, you really should. You never do anything for yourself. You're always doing something for others; you need to get a bike and go." I looked at her and said (with equal respect), "Are you crazy, too?" This was sometime in June.

I decided to take the motorcycle license course at the Harley dealership in Orlando, because it had been so long since I had done any riding. Just the little bit of being on the bike in class made me know I wanted to ride again.

Well, on July 6, Boodan and I went out looking and I almost bought a used Harley Road King. Something about it didn't feel right, so I changed my mind. I should have bought it, because while Boodan was in Sturgis, I bought a new 883 Sportster. Boodan would have never let me make that mistake. If you don't understand the mistake, ask a biker.

I bought the bike in Melbourne and was uncomfortable riding it to Orlando with so little experience. So, I rode it to Cocoa Beach and locked it in Boodan's garage (I had keys to his place). I would go over every day and ride up and down A1A for awhile. I left it in the garage until Boodan got back and then took it home. I rode it home on August 10, 2004.

I rode it to work the next day so Boodan and I could go for a ride together that afternoon. I didn't have a windshield yet and I wasn't wearing a helmet or goggles, so if I went over 55 mph, I couldn't see because the wind was whipping around my glasses and making my eyes water.

We rode up I-95 and ended up in Mims, which is a small town north of Titusville. We went to see Booger's little baby girl. Booger was another Warlock and one of Boodan's best friends. He was incarcerated at the time, but Boodan wanted me to meet his little Boogette. I had the opportunity to help Booger with a problem after he got out, but before I had the chance to know him well, or ride with him, I moved away from the area in 2005 to the southwest coast of Florida. My last opportunity to serve Booger was to perform his memorial service in 2008 after he was killed working on high-power lines.

A few days later I rode to work again. I had gotten a helmet with a face shield to deal with the watering eyes until I could get a windshield. Well, that afternoon, as I walked out of the hospital, the sky looking north and west was as black as it could be. Guess which direction I was going? Oh, you're good! I looked south toward Melbourne and it looked a lot better, so I decided to head south and west and hoped the storm was moving north. Wrong!

I got on I-95 and by the time I got to Highway 192 in Melbourne, which was my exit, it had started to rain. I got off and pulled into a convenience store to wait out the storm. How'd that go? Well, yea, I guess you know.

The storm didn't seem to be going anywhere, but the rain had slacked off a little, so I headed home. I found out later, this was just a trick to get me back out on the bike. Storms are like that.

Within a few minutes, the storm was raging again, huge claps of thunder and lightning…real close lightning. I had no rain gear, so I was soaked to the skin and freezing. This was before 192 was improved, so it was this narrow little, pot hole filled, two lane road with way too much traffic. By the way, trucks and cars hardly notice a storm, they just drive right on at highway speeds, seemingly unaware that you are about to die.

Have you ever been driving your car and have a eighteen wheeler run through a massive puddle in the other lane and have that huge wave of water wash over your windshield, suddenly making it impossible to see, until the wipers catch up? Now, just for a moment, close your eyes and imagine being on a motorcycle...ahhhh...refreshing! Did I mention the eighteen wheels? Yea, all nine on your side run through the same puddle. It comes close to washing you off your bike and off the road. Pretty scary for an inexperienced rider, I must say.

I confess that during this time I cursed my motorcycle. I couldn't believe I had let Boodan and Candy talk me into this. My full intention was to sell it as soon as...wait, the rain stopped... the sun came out. Suddenly, I was thinking, "That wasn't so bad...I can handle this."

Wait...oops, rain again...why did I let Boodan and Candy talk me into this...wait...sun. This experience happened several times on the way home. When I finally got home, I was shivering so bad, I had to get into a hot bathtub to try to warm my core.

But, I was hooked.

CHAPTER 45--
HOW I STARTED
RIDING--THE END

The first time I rode with the Warlocks was for the funeral of one of the brothers. Wayne "Hed" Nardella was killed in a motorcycle crash and his funeral was in Orlando on Saturday, September 25, 2004. I called Boodan and requested he ask Big John (who was the Cocoa chapter boss and is now the National President) if I could ride with them to the funeral. He said for me to meet them where the Beeline meets the 417. Boodan called to tell me when they left Cocoa and I rode out and waited on the side of the road. It was drizzling rain that day and I still did not have rain gear. Hurricane Jeanne was off the east coast.

The Warlocks rode past me at 90 miles an hour and waved for me to join them…thanks a lot. My little 883 Sportster would only do 100 at top end. It took me a few minutes to catch them going 100 on a rain slick highway. I thought to myself, "No wonder you guys get killed riding your motorcycles."

Do you remember how scared I said I was in that first ride home in the storm? Well, this was a whole new level of scared. This was check your pants scared. When I finally caught them, I was able to slow down to 90 and actually felt a little better.

As we got off the interstate and travelled through town, a couple of the brothers would move into intersections and block traffic while we all went through together, red light or not. Pretty neat! We finally arrived safely at the Orlando clubhouse. After spending some time at the wake with the brothers, my pager went off telling me that "Plan D" (D for disaster) had been called at the hospital, which meant Hurricane Jeanne was expected to hit and I needed to get to the hospital within the next few hours with plans to stay a day or two until Plan D was over. Candy was working in Bradenton and was staying at a hotel for a couple of days, so I didn't have to worry about her.

I had no idea where I was in Orlando. I had not paid any attention as we rode in (See Chapter 19), and it took me awhile, in another drizzling rain, to find my way back to a road I recognized so I could get home and then drive my car to the hospital.

I had to miss the funeral procession of 100 or more motorcycles riding to the cemetery for the services for Hed. I looked at the pictures later on the Warlocks web site. You can still see them here: www.warlocksmcorlando.net/HEDS_RIDE.html. This picture shows my little blue Sportster sticking out like a sore thumb: www.warlocksmcorlando.net/images/hedsmemorial44.jpg. I'm not sure who was riding that turquoise bike in the background.

The memory of that little blue bike helped me several years later after I had moved to southwest Florida. Dan Robertson and I rode to Cocoa for some business I had to do and before we headed home that night, we stopped by the Warlocks' Cocoa clubhouse because I wanted to pay respect and speak to Big John. It was the night for their club meeting and only members were allowed in. When Dan and I rode up to the gate, I realized I didn't know any of the new probates standing guard. They just looked at us suspiciously. Fortunately, they opened the gate for a brother to ride in and someone from inside saw me and yelled, "Hey Padre, you finally got rid of that blue bike." It was a brother who remembered me, maybe because of that little blue bike. Whew!

We were escorted into the club house and someone took me into a back room to see Big John. Dan was left in the main room, not knowing anyone and feeling pretty uneasy. After a few minutes, Big John and I came out and he met Dan and everyone knew we were okay. We left and when we stopped to get some gas and coffee, Dan said, "I was pretty scared when you left me by myself. People kept looking at me and all I kept saying was, 'I'm with Padre.'"

Well, the reason the brother noticed I finally got rid of that blue bike was I had bought a Harley Road King. It's black. Here's how that came about.

I was tired of riding the Sportster to work and back on the Beeline for 45 minutes each way. The sports suspension was beating me to death. So, I went by the Harley shop and was looking at a 2004 Police edition Road King. I liked the Police bike because of how the bags opened. Anyway, I put $1000 down on a new bike and when I got home, I called Big John to ask him what stuff I should have the Harley shop do before I brought the bike home. He said, "Padre, you should get you money back. I just talked with a guy today who has a 2003 Road King cop bike for sale. He's getting divorced and has to sell cheap. He's already done a lot of stuff to it." I followed that advice and on January 13, 2005, I bought that bike and rode it home.

I really didn't ride a lot for awhile. I wore a dress suit at the hospital, so on days I wanted to ride, I had to change clothes when I got to work and before I rode home. Also, it rains almost every afternoon somewhere on the Beeline. As you've already heard, rain takes some of the fun out of riding. It's still fun, but just not as fun. So, because of these things, I only rode in the evenings and weekends.

Oh well, watch for THE END--PART 2

CHAPTER 46--
HOW I STARTED RIDING-
-THE END--PART 2

I mentioned that I bought the Road King in January of 2005. On February 20th I rode over to Cocoa Beach to meet Boodan so we could ride to Daytona for the race. We had gone together for the Pepsi 400 in July of 2003 after Keith had died.

On the first one, I was unaware that it was a night race and got home to Orlando around 2:00 am and had to preach the next morning at Grace United Methodist Church in Merritt Island, which is over by Cocoa Beach. I didn't remember much about that sermon after I preached. I remember feeling like I was preaching in slow motion. I used to preach off the cuff without notes back then, so an awake, quick mind was a necessity. Guess what I didn't have that morning?

When I rode over for the February 20th race in 2005, it was one of those cold mornings in Florida. I was headed over at 6:00 am and it was dark and in the 40's. I know that doesn't sound cold to you northern riders, but to a Florida boy, yikes. It was much warmer when I got on Cocoa Beach, but when we headed up I-95 toward Daytona, it was miserable again. But, as you know, misery loves company, so it wasn't as bad as riding alone. We rode up at 90 mph. It got nice during the day but we had a cold ride home.

I think that was the last time we rode together. I moved to Englewood, Florida in August of 2005. Boodan has tried to get me to ride to Sturgis almost every year, but it hasn't happened yet. Bucket list anyone?

It wasn't until I moved to Englewood that I started riding everyday. As an assistant pastor, I do a lot of the visitation, especially in the hospitals. This means I get to ride 12 miles to Venice, 30 to Sarasota, 20 to Port Charlotte, 26 to Punta Gorda on a regular basis to visit. At times I get to ride 50 miles to Fort Myers, 70 to St Pete or 100 miles to Tampa General. The church pays my salary and gas. What a job!

The other pastors "have to drive" to those places; I "get to ride." It's a whole different mentality. I also get to stop by various "establishments of refreshment and entertainment for bikers" on my way back.

When I arrived at the church, we wondered how the church would react to a motorcycle riding pastor. Wow! They loved having a biker pastor. The business administrator, Dick Ringfelt, rode his bike to work everyday, so they were used to a motorcycle.

One Sunday, I walked up to a guy in the fellowship hall who looked like he might ride and asked him. He said that he did and I told him we might need to ride together sometime. He says that it's the only reason he came back after coming just to please his wife. They are a big part of the church now.

Not only did we find bikers, some who use to ride decided to ride again. Ted Hutchins has pictures of his mom and dad riding a 1929 Indian with his mom riding side-saddle since women didn't wear trousers back then. He grew up with motorcycles. He bought a small Suzuki to ride.

Dick Ringfelt came to me one day and said, "Herb, I think we need to start a monthly ride to see how many bikers we have." Our first ride on January 20, 2007 had 14 bikes and 19 people. As people invited friends, the group has grown. We have taken a monthly ride ever since then.

On September 22, 2007, Dick knew that it was Ted Hutchins' 87th birthday. He called the newspaper, hoping they would come to do an article about an older rider. We didn't know that Ted would show up that day with a brand new Harley that he bought himself for his birthday. It was a great article. Ted rode with us until he was about to turn 90 and decided it was time to stop. I attended his 90th party this week.

Anyway, we have a number of families that are a part of the church because of the motorcycle rides. They come to ride at the invitation of a friend. Then they find out that we're not as weird as they thought church people were; at least not weird in the way they thought church people were. They come to see what kind of church would have a pastor like me and they feel accepted and at home. It's really a great place.

Boodan came down to visit one weekend when I was preaching. It was communion Sunday and I asked him to assist with serving communion. He asked if I would get in trouble or something. I assured him it was okay. He served with my wife, Candy. It was a powerful moment for him and those he served.

It's just a glimpse into the journey that we are on and where it might be taking us.

CHAPTER 47--
YOU DON'T WANT
TO KNOW

his is a sermon I preached on July 16, 2006 at Englewood United Methodist Church, in Englewood, Florida. It's entitled, "You Don't Want to Know" and was taken from Acts 1:1-8.

Did you read the title of today's sermon? "You don't want to know." That's not the real title; it's just the working title. I thought they would put it on the sign out front and I didn't want the real title to scare you away.

The real title for today, if I had one, would be something about witnessing. See, I told you; some of you are ready to leave now. Most of us hate to hear sermons about witnessing. They make us feel terrible. I think it's because we have misunderstood it. Unfortunately, what has often been called witnessing is really personal evangelism. It's hard for most of us to do personal evangelism. Not many of us have the gift of evangelism, and it is truly a gift, therefore we are not involved in that level of sharing. Many of those with the gift of evangelism act like it's so easy to do and they try to make everyone else think they should be doing it, too, and if they're not, they should feel guilty. So, most of us spend our time feeling guilty that we are not witnessing.

You can't imagine the number of classes, conferences and seminars I've been to that involve people trying to train me to witness. What they're really training for is personal evangelism. Personal evangelism is basically preaching to one or two people. It's not even easy for a pastor to do that.

One young pastor learned what it's like trying to preach to just a few. He was asked by a funeral director to hold a grave-side service for a homeless man. He had no family or friends, and had died while traveling through the area. The funeral was to be held at a new cemetery way back in the country, and this man would be the first to be laid to rest there. The young pastor was not familiar with the backwoods area and became lost. He finally arrived an hour late. He saw the backhoe, and the crew who were eating lunch, but the hearse was nowhere in sight. He apologized to the workers for his tardiness, and stepped to the side of the open grave, where he saw the vault lid already in place. He assured the workers he would not hold them long, but this was the proper thing to do. The workers gathered around, still eating their lunches, and the young pastor poured out his heart and soul. As he preached the workers began to say "Amen," "Praise the Lord," and "Glory." This inspired the pastor who preached like he had never preached before. He closed the lengthy service with a prayer and walked to his car. He felt he had done his duty for the homeless man and that the crew would leave with a renewed sense of purpose and dedication, in spite of his tardiness. As he was opening the car door, he overheard one of the workers saying to another, "I ain't never seen anything like this before... and I've been puttin' in septic tanks for over twenty years."

Personal evangelism is opening the scripture or using scripture from memory and explaining the gospel to someone. Being a witness is not the same thing. The dictionary gives this definition of a witness: "One who can give a firsthand account of something seen, heard, or experienced." If being a witness is sharing a firsthand account, you can't be a witness of anything in the Bible. You have not seen, heard, or experienced any of those things.

If you are trying to explain scripture to someone who doesn't believe that the Bible is the Word of God, you're in trouble. You first have to figure out how to convince them of the truth of the Bible before you can share it with them. Try telling someone who doesn't believe the Bible that Mary was a virgin when Jesus was born, or that Jesus raised Lazarus from the dead. None of that makes any sense to someone who doesn't believe it. You cannot prove God or the Bible to anyone. But, what you can share is your story; what you have experienced. People have no way to dispute what you have experienced. It is real to you.

There's the old story of a Welch miner who was saved during a revival. He went back to the mines and told his friends he had become a believer. They made fun of him and asked how he could believe that Jonah was swallowed by a whale, or that Jesus walked on water or that he turned water into wine. The miner thought for a moment and then replied, "I don't know about all that. But I know that for me He turned whiskey into food for my family and shoes for my children." That's all he needs to know. And really, that's all he can tell. That's his story.

What's yours? You have a story, and people need to hear it. Your story is about how God changed your life. It's about being forgiven. It's about the things He has done in your life since then. It's about what He's done today. It's about answers to prayer. It's about struggles He's brought you through. It's about doubts and fears in the midst of your faith. Your story doesn't have to be all neat and clean and victorious, but it does have to be real, and it has to be yours.

Some of you may be thinking, "But pastor, where can I tell my story? I'm always with other Christians." I'll admit this becomes a real problem for some people. Your family is Christian and your friends and even acquaintances are people from church. And most of us grew up being taught not to be seen in places or with people that might hurt our reputations. That's interesting when we also talk about being Christ-like. Paul says of Jesus in Philippians 2:7, "But he made himself of no reputation." In Luke 7:34, Jesus says of himself, "The Son of Man has come eating and drinking, and you say, 'Look, a glutton and a drunkard, a friend of sinners!'" Jesus had a terrible reputation!

I'm afraid some of us are more concerned with our reputations than we are about caring for others. When Paul wrote to Timothy about choosing overseers for the church, he wrote, "He must also have a good reputation with outsiders." With outsiders? Today, we are not concerned with outsiders. Most of us are concerned with how others in the church see us. We're concerned with insiders, not outsiders. Let me tell you, from my experience, outsiders are not concerned with the same kind of reputation that your church friends are. Outsiders are not concerned about where you go or what you do; they are concerned about whether you care or not. That's the reputation they are looking for, and you can't care about them if you refuse to be around them.

When you look at Jesus' life in scripture, you often see him at dinners or parties in the home of a sinner. The religious leaders are standing on the porch looking in saying, "What's he doing in there? He's not supposed to be in there. He can't be religious and be with them and their kind. He can't be at their party and stay clean." But He could, and so can you.

One of my favorite stories of Jesus is when he met Zacchaeus. Luke 19:5-10 says, "Then Jesus entered and walked through Jericho. There was a man there named Zacchaeus, who was the head tax man and quite rich. He wanted desperately to see Jesus, but the crowd was in his way because he was a short man and couldn't see over them. So he ran on ahead and climbed up in a sycamore tree so he could see Jesus when he came by.

When Jesus got to the tree, he looked up and said, "Zacchaeus, hurry down. Today is my day to be a guest in your home." Zacchaeus scrambled out of the tree, hardly believing his good luck, delighted to take Jesus home with him. Everyone who saw the incident was indignant and grumped, "What business does he have getting cozy with this crook?"

Zacchaeus just stood there, a little stunned. He stammered apologetically, "Master, here and now I give away half of my possessions to the poor, and if I have cheated anyone, I will pay back four times the amount." Jesus said, "Today salvation has come to this home! Here he is: Zacchaeus, son of Abraham!"

Who invites you into their home? Whom do you invite into yours? Friends, that's who. Welcoming someone into your house is significant. It means acceptance of who they are, but not necessarily what they do. But in this case, just acceptance gave Zacchaeus the freedom to change. Sometimes that's all it takes.

Most of you know I ride a motorcycle. Not all of you know how that came about. One of our nurses had a son die who was a member of a motorcycle club. Some people use the term gang, but it's really a club. When he died, I became involved with his family through my connections with his mom. Because of this, I became friends with several of the brothers in the motorcycle club. They always showed me great respect and appreciated that I had included them in the funeral service. They began to ask me to come to different events at the clubhouse. They started calling me "Padre," a nickname I had been given at a marina when I lived on a sailboat for a couple of years. A brother would call and ask me to visit if any of the members came into the hospital, or if any of their family members came in. Recently one of the brothers was having surgery over in Cocoa Beach and another brother called me in Englewood to ask if I would call and pray with him before he went into surgery. Interesting, huh? While hanging out with these guys, they get to tell me the stories of their life and I get to tell them mine. That's one of the important parts of spending time with people, or just hanging out. You gain the privilege of telling your story by being willing to listen to theirs. By the way, most of my best life stories include God.

One brother in particular, called Boodan, began calling me for lunch or dinner just to spend time together. Through that time together and some rather interesting circumstances (which is another story), he has become one of my and my family's best friends. Why? Because he's a special person and we accept him just the way he is. We aren't trying to change him. If God wants him to change, that's God's business. My part is to love him and accept him. That's easy to do, we like him, too. He's trustworthy, loyal and fun. Friendship, love, and unconditional acceptance will give God a much greater chance to work than me trying to tell him what's wrong with his life. He already knows what's wrong with his life, just like I know what's wrong with mine and just like you know what is wrong with yours. You don't need me telling you where you fail; you live with that every day and night, just like I do. Neither do you need me telling you that you're okay just like you are. What you do need is for me to tell you that you're loved and accepted just like you are. You need me to do more than that; you need me to show you. So does everyone else in the world.

By the way, Candy and I called Boodan's mother one year on his birthday to tell her how much we loved and respected her son. She cried. She said, "Not many people get close enough to know his heart; they're turned away by how he looks, he looks scary." Jesus gets that close, doesn't he? Why shouldn't we?

I still hang out sometimes at places and with people you might question. Even so, I'm not suggesting that all of you should stop by

Will's Honky Tonk after church today (it's not big enough for everybody, anyway). I just want you to know that you don't have to preach to someone to be a witness. I want you to know how important your spiritual story is to those in your world whose own stories are filled with guilt, anger, and failure. The possibility that forgiveness can become a part of their story is good news to them. Hey, isn't that what the word gospel means? Good news? You bet it is!

CHAPTER 48--
THE F-WORD

When my son, Scott, was in pre-school, he came home one day and proudly announced to his mom that "he knew what the F-word was." Heartbroken at his loss of innocence at such an early age, she asked him what it was. He leaned over and whispered, "French fry."

That was his second encounter with the F-word. At an even earlier age, we were out to lunch with my parents, who were visiting from South Carolina. We were getting hamburgers at Krystal. I love those little square gut-bombs...a term of affection. They were an essential part of middle-of-the-night fare after sneaking out of the dorm in Nashville.

We'll talk about the importance of Krispy Kreme some other time. Go ahead and admit it; some of you remember when even the boys' dorms had a curfew.

Anyway, Dad and I were at the counter ordering while Kathy, Scott and Mom waited for us at a table. Scott was sitting beside his Grandma and across from Kathy. He was a very smart little kid and started reading something that had been written on the table. Kathy was listening, but not reading along since the word was upside down for her. Scott pronounced the sound of an F, and then the sound of a U, paused for a moment to figure out the combination letters, and then before Kathy could stop him, he finished with the K sound and proudly shouted out the word. If my mom had false teeth, she surely would have swallowed them. Kathy calmly told Scott, "That was very good reading, but that's not a word we use." "No, it's certainly not," my mom choked out. Kathy was still laughing when Dad and I made it back to the table.

If you want to shock people, just yell out the F-word, like Scott did, in an inappropriate place. It is interesting that a word could be considered so improper to use that it is given an alias. It's like "not speaking the name of God." Well, if you're not going to speak it, you have to make up a word that people will know means the same thing. Years ago, before people started using God or Jesus as exclamations, they used gosh or gee-whiz to vent their frustration.

I love F-words. Often, when I am saying the prayer before a meal, I will thank God for family, food, fellowship and fun. But those really aren't F-words, are they? They might be little f-words, but they are just words that begin with the letter f. A real F-word is one that people might not want to say out loud or with certain people. It is a word that is charged with such meaning that it can shock.

My F-word is Forgiveness. It isn't used much in everyday language these days or around certain people. It is charged with emotion even if not used in a religious context. Just hearing the word forgiveness indicates that someone has done something that they need to be forgiven for. Hearing it makes us uncomfortable; gives us the heebie-jeebies.

I think that a part of our hesitation to use the word forgiveness is that we all know how hard it is to really forgive someone. Oh, we might let it go or try to act like it never happened, but that's not the same as forgiveness. Is it? We also know how hard it is to ask for forgiveness from someone we've hurt or wronged. It is a humbling experience. There's an H-word for you.

If you need to forgive someone, you know what it does to you; you can't get away from the hurt or anger, and it just festers. That's a great word to describe it, too, festers. It gets worse and hurts more as time goes on. Forgiveness gets the poison out and allows healing to take place.

It is a different feeling if you've done something to someone and need to say, "I'm sorry." Rather than anger, there is regret and guilt, and you are always trying to avoid them. Asking for forgiveness will end those feelings even if the other person won't forgive you. It hasn't healed the relationship, but you've done all you can. They become the ones who must deal with it now. Or sometimes you find that they have already forgiven you because they did not want to carry around the hurt.

You never knew and you have been living with guilt for no reason. You just needed to receive their forgiveness to heal the relationship, it was there all along.

That's how it is with God's forgiveness. He's already forgiven us and all we need to do is accept it. Sounds easy, doesn't it. It is.

Real forgiveness has amazing power. It has the power to restore broken relationships, the power to lift huge feelings of guilt, the power to change life. Whether we need forgiveness from someone else, from God, or from ourselves (there's a tough one), forgiveness is profound. It brings acceptance and the chance for another F-word, Freedom. Freedom gives us a chance to change and to live life in the everyday giving and receiving of Forgiveness.

Go ahead, shout it out and shock somebody!

"My F-Word is Forgiveness" is Herb Agee's first book. His warmth, wit and wisdom are a combination of best friend, companion, pastor, brother, and humorist – with emphasis on humorist. From "Groceries, Outhouses and Chewing Tobacco" to "The F-Word," Agee leads the reader on a roller coaster ride of shared human experiences and emotions. As a former hospital chaplain, police officer and church pastor for many years, he has shared life and death on deep personal levels with thousands. Presently an assistant pastor at Englewood United Methodist Church in Englewood, Florida, Agee rides a Harley and hangs out with the local bikers and goes by the nickname, Padre. He also has a website with a unique concept ministry, www.StFrancisHelps.com.

Through vignettes, observations, musings and ramblings, Agee goes from the heights of hilarity to the peace and quiet of introspection. The real life application approach to the observations and autobiographical experiences are based upon the author's beautifully simplistic approach to life, living and loving. Agee's appeal extends beyond gender and age to touch the heart and sense of humor of all. "My F-Word is Forgiveness" is a book for every reader.